Casey weaves a modern parable in a fast-moving rendition of the *Titanic* and an honest view of church leadership styles. From a page in history, a warning instructs the Church of today. For him who has ears to hear, let him hear.

—*Joel E. Shirk, Pastor, Christ Community Church, Cheshire, CT*

Here is a burst of revelation that has been locked in the depths of the Atlantic waters of our understanding until now. Both the positive and negative actions and reactions in this fascinating story are presented with great clarity. In the reading of this we can all learn very valuable lessons to help us avoid the pitfalls and utilize the wisdom that Casey has discovered.

—*Leon Carter Price, Pastor, Washington, DC*

A convicting, penetrating, and sobering insight into church leadership with a call for change and repentance. We must stop looking at each other and evaluate our own lives in the face of this prophetic challenge.

—*Robert Van Meter, Pastor, Vineyard Christian Fellowship, Prospect, CT*

Titanic
Warning

Hearing the Voice of God
in This Modern Age

Titanic Warning

Hearing the Voice of God in This Modern Age

by
Casey Sabella

New Leaf Press

First Edition
October 1994

ISBN: 0-89221-271-3
Library of Congress: 94-68851

Cover: Painting © Ken Marschall from *Titanic: An Illustrated History,* a Madison Press/Hyperion book, painted from data supplied by Dr. Robert Ballard.

The sea gave up the dead that were
in it . . . and each person was judged
according to what he had done
(Rev. 20:13).

*Dedicated to the body of Christ
for her edification, exhortation,
and comfort*

Acknowledgements

Thanks are due to many for their help, encouragement, and insight:

The Titanic Historical Society who for more than 30 years have pursued every detail of the most fascinating maritime disaster in history. Their labors have made research considerably easier for me in every way.

Ray Lepien, vice president of the Titanic Historical Society looked my manuscript over and made helpful suggestions.

Don Lynch was gracious enough to assist a fellow writer out, though the history recorded in these pages is, at best, only a copy of the work he has so painstakingly done.

Ken Marschall, whose brilliant paintings have made that terrible night in April vivid for us all. Thank you for the haunting image that appears on the cover of this book, and for making your collection and knowledge available to us.

Ann House of the Steamship Historical Society of America, and *Charlotte Valentine* and *Tom Crew* of the Mariners Museum, for their selfless and generous gathering of the photographs in this book.

My parents for the two things writers seldom get but always need: enthusiasm and support.

Our local church, for the patient and loving care they give me daily. I am privileged to serve with these brothers and sisters in the gospel.

Finally, to *Patricia,* my lovely bride, and the *four best children* a man could ever hope for. You continue to bring me the sweetest joy.

Contents

Foreword

I've been in ministry for 36 years. During the past 24 years I have helped start churches all over the United States, Canada, Mexico, and other parts of the world. I've ministered in many denominational, non-denominational, Charismatic, Pentecostal, and Evangelical churches, spending time with leaders from many different parts of the world.

After reading the manuscript of *Titanic Warning,* I believe it is a prophetic word to the Church, and I'm convinced that it is really a warning. Most of us know that a great shaking is taking place in the Church. Now there is a book to help us see where we are in leadership. This book, if read and prayed about, can change what we've been doing for years.

In Judges it says that before Gideon could go to battle, he had to tear down his father's altars to Baal. *Titanic Warning* will help us see that we have built many altars that really aren't from God. They are simply things we have built.

Scripture says the gates of hell shall not prevail against His church, yet many churches have fallen: either we did not build as God wanted or we let pride get into it so God had to let it go. Many times we have declared that it was the work of the enemy, when all along it was God allowing it to happen to reveal what we were really doing. I pray that as this book is read we will truly repent so we may see what God is saying. How does He want His church built? How does He want leaders to act? *Titanic Warning* will help us come to a better understanding of what the Church is to be. I believe Brother Casey has heard the Lord who is warning us to stop and examine the way we are building.

I hope, pray, and believe that we can change, and it will be a change for what God wants, not what man wants.

—Bob Terrell
President, Foundation Ministries

Prologue

In the wake of the sinking of the *Titanic,* churches on both sides of the Atlantic were filled to overflowing. The disaster had slapped the face of a sleeping world, and parishioners sat, blinking and wide-eyed, as ministers tried to put it all in perspective. The following excerpts from sermons in the United States reflect the general mood during the second half of April 1912.

If the builders of the *Titanic* had had a real faith in the almightiness of God, they would not have believed that they could build something to master His seas. It was science they called upon, science, which since the days of Martin Luther, has grown to be the mentor of the world. It gave them swimming pools, elevators, gorgeous suites, and promenades, every comfort that a depraved and luxurious nation loves. But science, which has brought the world between us and God, can never produce anything that will not crumple at the touch of God.

—Rev. Charles A. Eaton
Madison Avenue Baptist Church
New York City
Sunday, April 21, 1912

It has sobered the world. As we celebrate the death of little children as martyrs on Holy Innocents' Day we will memorialize those who sank on the *Titanic* as the martyrs of this age sacrificed by God to arouse the world to a deeper spiritual realization, to a desire for a more splendid type and a consciousness that life is ever ending and we must be prepared to meet death when it comes. In the risen Christ we find promise of that life to come, not only for those who have gone before but for those who remain.

> —Dean Sumner
> Episcopal Cathedral
> Chicago
> Sunday, April 21, 1912

Introduction

Stepping aboard the plane, I made my way down the aisle. The small aircraft would carry me from Connecticut to Texas after a stopover in Nashville, Tennessee. Due to a last-minute scheduling problem, a pastor friend of mine provided this all-expenses-paid trip to a leaders' conference in the once oil-rich city of Houston. I looked forward not only to this brief hiatus from the cold New England weather, but also an opportunity to use a notebook computer I'd rented from the local PC store.

Seated next to me was a mother from Phoenix, Arizona, who was flying home with her family. Her young daughter sat next to her, while her husband supervised their son several rows in front of us. After introducing myself, I sat down for what would prove to be an interesting flight.

While we listened to the stewardess explain emergency procedures, I became distracted by the picture on the front cover of a novel my fellow passenger was reading. Could it be? No, this was too coincidental! Here I was, onboard to finish writing a book on the *Titanic*, and this lady was reading a fictional story about two star-crossed lovers who survived it!

As a Christian, I know these coincidences are a regular part of life. Believers learn to pay attention when such things occur because God often uses coincidences to reveal His will or provide guidance.

I asked this young mother a few questions, attempting to seize the opportunity God was evidently providing. Perhaps I would be permitted the privilege of sharing the gospel. Never happened — though I did manage to uncover every detail about her you could ask (and I should have stopped asking after the first question!) Throughout the entire flight she never stopped talking about her husband, his first wife, their children, her superior home state, their house, and most importantly, herself. I was dumbfounded! Though her husband served as a deacon in a Christian church at one time, it was obvious that Jesus was not the center of their lives.

Thankfully, my writing project enabled me to escape this one-way conversation for a time, though she continued to talk.

When the plane finally landed, I had collected enough information about her to write another book (it wouldn't have sold many copies)! On the other hand, what little she learned about me had been volunteered. She never asked a question; never inquired of my family, job, interests, or final destination.

Two hours later, I boarded the plane scheduled to transport me from Nashville to Houston. Still mystified by the previous encounter, I started down the center aisle to seat 9D. Seated beside me on this occasion was an old woman from India. Upon her lap was a rectangular wooden box. Upon her forehead, a red dot. That could only mean one thing: she was a Hindu.

Thankfully, she spoke a little English. Having spent two weeks in India many years before, I had a point of reference to initiate conversation. She was returning from a visit with one of her children, having lived in the United States for several years. She attempted to answer other questions, but appeared to be nursing a serious cough. I attempted to assist her with water, cough drops, etc.

When the plane began to descend, I prepared myself for the dynamics of disembarking. My thoughts focused upon finding my way to the baggage claim area and then securing a taxi driver to take me to the hotel.

When we landed, I said goodbye to my fellow second passenger and headed for the escalator area. Minutes later this same woman spied me struggling with my luggage. She came over and introduced me to her son, Raj, who worked for the NASA Space Center in Houston. When they learned where I would be staying, Raj insisted on giving me a ride. I thanked him for his hospitality, surprised at how considerate he was toward a virtual stranger.

The hotel was not two miles away (as I had been told), but seven. "No problem," replied Raj as he tossed my bags in the trunk. With Mom and her box in the back seat, we snaked our way through Houston traffic at eleven o'clock at night, talking, laughing, and sharing.

What did we talk about? Mostly family-related issues. Raj couldn't understand, for example, why American teenagers dream of leaving home. In India, families live together for life — several generations mentoring and caring for each other all their days. Why was it, he wanted to know, that Americans desire independence so badly? Was not this desire to leave home one of the chief causes of our alarming divorce rate? Raj's questions were penetrating and inescapable as we looked at the principles of raising family and children India-style vs. American-style. I could only affirm that his observations were accurate in many ways.

I was able to share with him the difference between the Christian faith of the Bible and present American culture. While we are founded upon many biblical principles, I told Raj, today's society reflects decidedly anti-Christian beliefs and practices.

When we arrived at the hotel, I helped Mom get out of the back seat. When I offered to hold the box, she refused. Raj told me that the box contained her god. (How's that for putting god in a box!) Raj insisted on carrying my bags into the lobby, and before leaving, scribbled down his home and work phone numbers, demanding I call him if any need arose. He also offered me free transportation wherever I might need to go during my stay. For the second time in the same night, I was dumbfounded at the attitude of a stranger.

Later on, while unpacking my bags and preparing for bed, I could not help reflecting on the unique contrast between these two families I had met. It was then that the Holy Spirit opened my understanding of His purposes in these two passengers.

The first passenger possessed a working knowledge of Jesus Christ. She displayed all the exterior appearances of Christianity, but was thoroughly self-absorbed. She did not perceive God's purposes for her existence beyond satisfying her own needs. Consequently, she had little time to invest herself into the life of another. The second passenger, while steeped in pagan beliefs, still managed to demonstrate more caring and visible Christian hospitality than many believers living in the United States today. This mother and son had been trained to serve others. They saw their existence to have wider significance than self-gratification. Hospitality occupied a large priority in their lives.

I believe that the Lord provided me with these passengers to confirm the theme of this book. You will have the opportunity to compare servants and the self-absorbed from an earlier age. God's heart is burdened with the church of America. The church has not grown numerically in more than a decade. Analysis of current church statistics show that many rapid-growth churches are largely the product of transfers (Christians moving from one church to another). True missions growth — due to the addition of unchurched people — averages at 5 percent. When you place this percentage alongside the population growth in our country, we are declining, not gaining ground, in reaching the lost of our nation.

Church leaders are stuck in mindsets and habit patterns that nullify their ability to reach the unchurched. Sunday after Sunday they preach their hearts out to small but loyal crowds of people who yawn much and change little. In their quiet times, these pastors of small churches (which represent the majority in the U.S.) ache with frustration. They are unable to perceive why their congregations do not grow in number or character.

A pastor's self-esteem is on the line every week in the pulpits of American churches. Feelings of self-worth rise or fall on who was present or absent, or whether the weekly offering amount was enough to cover current expenses. When the sermon has impact, he is congratulated. When it flops, people superfluously smile as they leave. The pastor's public performance may be over for another Sunday — but another will be required in a few short days. Then emotions will again be taken for a roller-coaster ride leaving him tired, depressed, and bewildered.

Society's evil is not the obstacle. The great revivals of other generations were birthed in much worse environments. Jesus' words in John 4:35 that "the harvest is ripe," have not changed. It remains ready and waiting. We may blame our failure on the lack of committed laborers, but this only partially explains our impotence.

We need to consider the laborers already on the harvest field. They are ill-equipped and poorly trained in biblical Christianity. Most haven't the vaguest idea of where the harvest is, what it takes to bring it in, or how to use the increase for an even greater harvest. We blame the crops, the tools we've been given, other laborers, the weather, and a host of other hindrances. Yet, the harvest in America remains largely ungathered because few church members have been discipled. We don't look to ourselves for blame.

It may be time to reassess the way we conduct church. We have worked at becoming better preachers, but our fruit doesn't look like Jesus. Why? Our society is hungry for God, but doesn't want what the Church is offering. Do we attribute this to the darkness of their pagan minds, or have we failed to visibly demonstrate Jesus of Nazareth to this spiritually voracious society?

This book is designed to challenge the premises upon which today's churches operate. Though we would all like to think that we are biblical in our approach to church life, most of us are surprisingly traditional. That is, we tend to do what we've seen others do rather than respond to God's specific direction for our ministries.

It is time to change. God desires that every member of the body of Christ function according to the blueprint He set forth long ago.

How and what do we change? The answer may not be as difficult to grasp as we might imagine.

Chapter 1

Nothing Can Go Wrong ... Go Wrong ... Go Wrong

While most of us were sleeping, Robert Ballard was making history. On September 1, 1985, at 1:40 a.m., Bob was relaxing in his flannel pajamas reading a book. The autobiography of Chuck Yeager provided a needed diversion, transporting his soul back through time and into the vastness of space thousands of feet above him. Another day of fruitless searching had passed. Weeks had become months with little progress to report to those who had invested millions of dollars into his dream. Until that moment, all Bob could show for his backbreaking labor was sand from the bottom of the cold North Atlantic.

When Johnny the cook sprang into the boss's room to tell him the news, Ballard's heart began pounding with intense excitement. Could this be the prize that had eluded so many before him? Would his crew of three dozen be rewarded for all their tedious and painstaking work?

One advantage they did have was the technical support financial backing afforded them. Employed by the Woods Hole Oceanographic Institute, Ballard and his team had the use of the U.S. Navy research vessel, *Knorr*. Aboard ship were ANGUS and ARGO, the latest in undersea camera systems to guide in the search.

Moments after hearing Johnny's startling news, the entire crew jammed into the control room. All eyes were fixed upon the television monitors where video images from ARGO revealed a man-made object resting on the ocean floor. The enormous cylindrical object had giant rivets and three stoking doors. There could be no doubt: it was a boiler! They were watching history in the making. Anxiously, the crew waited to see the sight no human had witnessed in 73 years.

ARGO's cameras continued scanning the ocean floor. There were copper pots and steel pans, tools, wine bottles with corks still in them, china in perfect condition, lumps of coal, and clothing in near-perfect condition. Like a detective following a trail, ARGO continued to search. That abruptly ended when the cameras revealed the bow of the most notorious ocean liner ever built: R.M.S. *Titanic*.

The boisterous celebration of triumph in the tiny control room that morning echoed the jubilation each crew member felt. Months of arduous work had finally paid off. Bob Ballard's 12-year personal quest for the *Titanic* was finally over, and the sense of accomplishment was overwhelming.

But then something unexpected happened. War cry hollers and satisfying laughter subsided to be replaced by an eerie silence. The faces of the crew lost their merriment. Smiles of moments before gave way to looks of great sobriety. As every eye watched the television monitor, all aboard shared the same thoughts. This was not only the most significant undersea find in the twentieth century, it was also the discovery of the gravesite where 1,522 people lost their lives during a night of profound terror.

Coincidentally enough, Ballard's expedition found the *Titanic* near the time of day she actually sunk. Knowing that the full realization of what they had discovered was being felt by all, Ballard led his team to the *Knorr's* stern. After raising the Harland and Wolff flag (from the Irish ship-building company), the crew observed a moment of silence on behalf of those who were drowned and frozen when the *Titanic* went down at 2:20 a.m.

News of the discovery traveled quickly. Newspapers and national magazines heralded the tidings with tremendous excitement. Ballard's expedition became famous overnight. However, several months would pass before Ballard recovered from what he termed a "mini-nervous breakdown." The trauma of being where so many had perished would haunt him for many days and nights. Bob's inability to express the depth of feeling he experienced made him somewhat aloof from friends and family. Instead of capitalizing on his discovery, Ballard withdrew from the world, canceling interviews with Tom Brokaw and Phil Donahue. In Ballard's own words:

"I never thought I'd go crazy over it. And sometimes I think I did go a little crazy. Finding the ship, I did not expect it to hit me in such a tragic sense. I did not expect to feel the disaster to the level I felt it. I was in tears. I must have looked like a real crybaby. I just — I was really depressed. And, believe me, I never expected that. I expected it to be the exact opposite. Instead, I wanted to run away from the *Titanic*. I wanted it out of my life. I didn't want to see a soul, to talk to a soul about the *Titanic*. I just . . . I haven't told these things to anyone outside my family. I still don't want to talk about it, for some odd reason — very painful. I can't explain it. I just — I . . . can . . . remember the reactions."[1]

Working on the next stage of investigating the *Titanic* was the only thing that kept Bob's mind from a continuing state of grief and mourning. Returning to the wreck in 1986, Ballard and his team took more than 50,000 pictures and logged 100 hours of videotape. The information they retrieved from viewing the shipwreck has enabled us to piece together what happened on that fateful night of April 14, 1912.

I have come to believe that the sequence of events that eventually culminated in the sinking of the world's most prestigious ocean liner in 1912 have astounding relevance to the church of Jesus Christ at this time in our history. Why the ship was built, her philosophy of operation, the methodologies influencing the decision-making process, weather conditions at the time, the classification of passengers, the experience of the crew, her overall design — all combine to present to us a unique picture of why today's Church is sinking when she should be triumphant.

The *Titanic* story is about paradigms. Paradigms are *mindsets*. They are lenses through which we view reality. Paradigms define the rules by which we live. Before Columbus, for example, Europeans were stuck in the paradigm that the world was flat. Though that theory was wrong, the majority of the world population believed it was true and lived their lives accordingly. All decisions regarding sea travel were governed by this paradigm.

This world-renowned ship went to the bottom decades ago because thousands of people put their faith in a paradigm: that she was "unsinkable." We will soon discover that many facets of her maiden voyage correspond directly to faulty paradigms that the Church has accepted as truth for centuries.

The *Titanic* also serves as a prophetic beacon. It points today's Christian to what the future will hold if we fail to make course corrections. The Church is traveling in the right direction for the wrong reason on the wrong ship. God is speaking, but too often we have not exerted the effort to listen. Ineffective church traditions have distracted us from listening to our Lord. Humility must replace pride if we will ever become the potent force in the earth to change the hearts of men.

The twentieth century Church has failed in her mission to disciple the nations. We have more Christians in America than ever before, but fewer disciples. The reasons for this are locked away in a massive hunk of steel on the floor of the Atlantic Ocean.

The Beginning or the End?

The story of the *Titanic* begins in 1858 when Edward James Harland purchased a shipyard situated at Queen's Island in Belfast, Northern Ireland. With his partner, Gustav Wolff, Harland set out to build a competitive and successful business.

Harland's successor joined the firm in 1862. A teenager at the time, Bill Pirrie gained experience as an apprentice drafter. Years later it was through Pirrie that Harland and Wolff underwent an ambitious modernization program (between 1906 and 1908). This moderniza-

Harland and Wolff, in Belfast, Northern Ireland — the shipyard where many ocean liners were built — as it appears in 1994.

tion enabled them to build increasingly larger ships, and become a force to be reckoned with in the shipping industry.

Beginning in the 1870s, Harland and Wolff constructed many ships for the White Star Line. At the turn of the century, they built the *Celtic* (1901), the *Cedric* (1903), the *Baltic* (1904), and the *Adriatic* (1907). Each ship was a masterpiece designed to exceed the size of its predecessor.

White Star's chief rival at the time was Cunard, a British line. Chiefly to match their two 790-foot ships, — *Lusitania* (1906) and *Mauretania* (1907) — White star proposed to build three liners, each 50 percent larger in overall space than their rival. They were to be named *Olympic, Titanic,* and *Gigantic* (*Gigantic* became *Britannic*, but we're getting ahead of ourselves).

At 882'5" long, the *Titanic* dwarfed all other liners. The rivets alone — weighing two million, four hundred thousand pounds — joined together a ship with a net weight of nearly 44 million pounds. Her rudder, like none ever seen, was six stories high!

Harland and Wolff spared no expense in building

The world's most luxurious ship being prepared for the maiden voyage. This view gives a good perspective of the incredible length of the ship. *(Courtesy of the Steamship Historical Society Collection, University of Baltimore Library)*

the *Titanic*. The finest materials combined with expert workmanship ensured she would be a phenomenon never witnessed in history. The Grand Saloon was gigantic in size with beautiful columns supporting exquisite wood sculpture. Carved walnut flowers ran from floor to ceiling. Ankle-deep oriental carpets, horse-hair sofas, silk lamp shades and crystal chandeliers made the *Titanic* seem more like a lavish hotel than a ship.[2]

She was the first ship to offer a full-size swimming

A second-class passenger room. This is actually from the *Olympic,* but the rooms were identical in almost every way to the *Titanic.*
(Courtesy of the National Maritime Museum, Greenwich, England)

pool for her guests. The *Titanic* also came equipped with Turkish baths, a full-size squash court, a verandah cafe with palm courts, tea gardens, smoking rooms, a gymnasium, a dark room for developing pictures, four passenger elevators, eight electric cargo cranes, and a 50-telephone switchboard.

In spite of this, one queer paradox existed. The *Titanic* had enough lifeboats for 1,178 people, while the ship could hold more than double that amount: 3, 511.[3] Antiquated regulations based on cubic linear footage by the Board of Trade Commission required lifeboat capacity to be just 962. And while her original plans called for as many as 48 lifeboats (more than adequate), she was finally equipped with 16 wooden lifeboats and four collapsibles. Though no expense had been spared to ensure luxury, the builders had cut costs on measures designed to save human life!

At her launching May 31, 1911, the *Titanic* commanded a breathtaking sight. The length of three football fields, she was awesome to behold. "Not even God himself could sink this ship," a crewman is said to have uttered. Such sentiments, repeated in one form or another, became transfixed in many minds as reality. The picture of elegance, she carried many of society's finest in her first class division. There were friends of the president, wealthy entrepreneurs, and men and women respected in art, science, and literature.

Down below, the *Titanic* carried immigrants in her third-class compartment. Anxious to visit relatives who had emigrated to the United States before them, families from all over Europe crowded aboard with the hope of beginning a new life. Amid tearful goodbyes, the *Titanic* moved away from the shores of Southampton, England.

A first-class stateroom. Note the smiling gentleman in the mirror. *(Courtesy of the Mariners' Museum, Newport News, Virginia)*

The promenade deck of the *Titanic*'s sister ship, the *Olympic*.
(SSHSA Collection, U of B Library)

Captain Edward John Smith of the *Titanic*. Smith, known as
"E.J." to his first-class passengers, was a 38-year veteran of
the sea, and planned to retire after the *Titanic*'s maiden
voyage. *(Courtesy of Grant Freeman)*

Once underway, she would reach a speed exceeding 22
1/2 knots (more than 24 1/2 land miles per hour).

Captain Edward J. Smith, affectionately known as
"E.J.," was an accomplished seaman. His career had been
illustrious, and at age 62 he was nearing retirement when
asked to become the *Titanic*'s skipper. Smith had commanded the *Olympic*, the *Titanic*'s smaller sister ship.

Less than a year earlier, the *Olympic* collided with
the naval cruiser *Hawke*, which punched a 20 cubic-foot

hole through her side. By closing the watertight compartments, the *Olympic* was rescued from sinking. Smith thought it was a miracle. This accident may have strengthened his feeling that these newer liners *were* unsinkable[4] (a belief propagated by the press). It was an age when people believed that technology could conquer all obstacles. Many believe that the *Titanic* was to be Captain Smith's final commission before retiring from White Star.

With the *Titanic* well underway, the passengers acquainted themselves with all of the nuances of life aboard ship. The initial strangeness of the surroundings gradually disappeared much like the coast they had left behind. All indications pointed to a delightful journey . . . until Saturday night at 10:30 p.m. The steamer *Rappahannock* was sighted traveling in the opposite direction. It signaled the *Titanic* by Morse lamp with the message: "Have just passed through heavy field ice and several icebergs." Passed through indeed, twisting her rudder and denting her bow! After pausing briefly, the *Titanic* replied by Morse lamp: "Message received. Thanks. Good night." An ominous warning, but no cause for alarm. Expert navigation would keep them out of difficulty, it was reasoned.

Eaton and Haas in their book, *Titanic, Destination Disaster*, described the atmosphere aboard ship on Sunday, April 14:

> In the saloons and smoking rooms there were rumors of a record crossing. Many passengers and, indeed, some crew believed the company wished to display its new liner in a most favorable light by bringing her across to New York with a new speed record.
>
> Sunday saw two breaks in shipboard rou-

RMS *Titanic* (*Courtesy of the Mariners' Museum, Newport News, Virginia*)

tine: there was no daily inspection of the vessel, and Divine Service was held. At 10:30 a.m. passengers from all classes convened in the first-class dining saloon. Led by Captain Smith, the service was not from the Church of England's *Book of Common Prayer,* but rather, from the company's own prayer book.

The day was bright and clear. During the afternoon it became noticeably cool. Passengers deserted the decks and sought comfort and warmth in the spacious lounge, the cozy library, or the comfortable smoking room. . . . In the first-class reading room — its floor carpeted in old rose, its windows hung with pink draperies — passengers leisurely read books and the latest magazines placed there by the *Times of London's* book club.

The library's quiet contrasted with the carnival atmosphere of the smoking room. Here there was no sea view: light entered through painted glass windows depicting landscapes, ancient ships, and historic and mythological figures. Over the marble fireplace hung a large oil painting, "Plymouth Harbour," by the well-known British painter Norman Wilkinson.

In the main lounge a trio from the ship's orchestra played the day's popular songs: music from operettas, the musical stage, or the new sensation, ragtime; salon pieces, reminiscent of a smart continental cafe; gems from Gilbert and Sullivan operettas "Mikado," "Pirates of Penzance;" and waltzes by Strauss."[5]

Early that morning, the *Titanic* picked up a wireless

message from the *Caronia,* traveling from New York to Liverpool, England. "Captain, *Titanic* — West-bound steamers report bergs, growlers, and field ice in 42 degrees North from 49 degrees to 51 degrees West. . . ." This second of six warnings was delivered to Captain Smith on the bridge. He read it and then posted it for his officers to read.

At 1:42 in the afternoon, the White Star liner *Baltic* relayed a message from the Greek steamer *Athinai*, warning of icebergs and field ice close to the *Titanic*'s expected course. In addition, the message relayed that the German oil tanker *Deutschland* was in trouble and short of coal in the *Titanic*'s vicinity. The message was handed to Smith, who did not immediately post it, but instead carried it with him toward A-deck. According to White Star executive J. Bruce Ismay (who survived), Smith handed him the message without saying a word. Ismay glanced at it, put it in his pocket, and went below. Five and one-half hours passed before it was posted for the officers to see.

The day turned to dusk and then to dark. The air temperature began to fall. Because of the day's telegraph messages, Captain Smith ordered crewmen to keep a sharp lookout for ice, but the liner never slowed down.

At 7:30 p.m. the telegraph officer overheard a message from the freighter *Californian* to the *Antillian*. Its message reported ice about 19 miles north of *Titanic*'s expected course. This message was not taken to Smith who was engaged at a dinner hosted by the Wideners.[6]

Outside, the sky was pitch-black on a moonless night. By 9:40 p.m. the air temperature had dropped to 33 degrees. John Phillips (the telegraph officer at the time) received a message from still another ship, the *Mesaba*. It reported "Much heavy pack ice and great number large icebergs. Also, field ice. Weather good, clear."

Phillips was busy transmitting messages to land for the passengers. He and his fellow wireless operator, Harold Bride, had spent seven hours that day fixing a burned-out relay. As a result, a mountain of messages from the passengers had piled up. Phillips chose to ignore the *Mesaba* message, and to this day no one is sure what became of it.

On an ocean smooth as glass, the *Titanic* raced towards her destiny. It appeared certain that she would outstrip her own expectations and arrive in New York well ahead of schedule. Wouldn't White Star be proud to see the *Titanic*'s picture emblazoned once again across the front pages of newspapers around the globe?

Minutes before 11:00 p.m. the final warning came from the *Californian*. The signal itself was loud, irritating Phillips who was still busy transmitting. The nearby ship reported: "We are stopped and surrounded by ice." Swamped with messages and angered by the interruption, Phillips telegraphed a message back: "Shut up. I am busy. I am working Cape Race" (messages from Cape Race, Newfoundland). The *Californian* continued trying to reach them for a half-hour and then gave up.

Outside, the air was cold. Fredrick Fleet and Reginald Lee had just 20 minutes left on their lookout watch. Though Fleet had requested them, there were no binoculars in the lookout's cage. The men were forced to rely on their senses to detect danger.

A moist, clammy smell filled the air. As he strained to see ahead in the moonless night, the stars began to disappear from Fred Fleet's sight. Could it be? An ice-blue wall appeared in front of him which brought horror to his face. Giving the cord on the bell three sharp pulls, Fleet then reached for the telephone, frantically calling James P. Moody on the bridge. "Iceberg right ahead!" he screamed.

First Officer William Murdoch took Moody's message and sprang into action. Ordering a "Hard-a-starboard!" and "Full speed astern!" Murdoch also told the engine room to close the watertight doors in the engine and boiler room bulkheads. The *Titanic* slowly steered away from the massive iceberg rising out of the water between 50 and 100 feet.

Fireman Fred Barrett had been hard at work stoking the furnaces in No. 6 boiler room. Foaming green sea water suddenly exploded through the *Titanic*'s side about two feet above the floor plates, shearing the starboard wall. Watertight compartments began to close, and Barrett just managed to jump through!

At first, few onboard were aware that a collision had taken place. Many passengers did not notice the impact, which lasted only 10 seconds. However, during those 10 seconds at top speed, the *Titanic*'s massive hull was bent inward, breaking seams and stabbing holes into her side underneath the waterline. The holes taken together opened up approximately 12 square feet — but they breached at least five compartments. Had it been only four, the *Titanic* could have limped to safety. Five signaled her doom.

Within minutes, the awakened Captain Smith came to the bridge and began receiving damage reports. The verdict: the *Titanic* had no chance of survival. Smith was now faced with an impossible dilemma. It was up to him to mobilize the orderly evacuation of the ship and save as many people as possible. The job of the captain and officers "would be difficult, not only because there were too few lifeboats, but because the *Titanic* had not put the passengers [nor crew] through a proper lifeboat drill."[7]

He ordered the wireless operators to issue a distress signal: "Come at once. We have struck a berg. It's a CQD (Come Quick, Danger), MGY (*Titanic*'s call letters). Positions 41'46' N, 50'14' W." The message was addressed to anyone who would listen. Fifty-eight miles away, a Cunard liner, the *Carpathia*, heard the call and changed course.

As for the *Titanic*, she had now slowed to a complete stop. The unsinkable ship — the pride of all the world — had a little over two hours before death.

Although the ship was not moving, the crew continued in their routines as if nothing was wrong. Stewards finished preparing breakfast tables that would be 13,000 feet underwater by daybreak.

Smith ordered the crew to stand by to uncover the lifeboats. However, few members of the crew had substantive training in doing so. No one had participated in an official lifeboat drill. Confusion and poor communication followed, causing many lives to be lost unnecessarily. The crew was ill-prepared to deal with helping passengers to abandon the ship. Precious minutes passed as disorganization prevented the boarding and the lowering of lifeboats.

As more of the bow continued to disappear each minute, 20 lifeboats were finally lowered, averaging 44 people each. Considering that the capacity of each was 65, we get an idea of how chaotic the process was. Quartermaster Rowe was the last person aboard to learn of the *Titanic*'s accident — an hour later! Captain Smith ordered him to fire the first distress rocket at 12:45 a.m. Seven more followed.[8]

Near the front of the liner, the orchestra played a lively set of tunes which helped keep the passengers calm. These brave men, under the leadership of bandmaster Wallace Hartley, played for the next hour and 20 minutes. Legend says that when Hartley advised his men that they had done their duty and could leave, no one moved. They stayed together, playing their instruments until seconds before the *Titanic* was submerged beneath the waves.

By 2:10 a.m., the water had filled too much of the ship for it to remain afloat. The bow slipped underwater first, arching the stern upward. The lights blacked out while tons of machinery crashed to the bow. Hundreds of screaming people were thrown into the icy sea. Higher and higher the *Titanic*'s stern rose into the air as the bow sank beneath the water. The enormous funnels broke off one at a time, sending clouds of soot and steam into the air.

Cries for help from those in the ocean were loud at first, then gradually subsided until there was silence. Charles Lightoller, a surviving member of the crew reported: "What I remember about that night — what I will remember as long as I live — is the people crying, 'I love you.' "[9]

Another survivor, Archibald Gracie, later testified in U.S. Senate hearings: "There arose to the sky the most horrible sounds ever heard by mortal man. The agonizing cries of death from over a thousand throats, the wails and groans of the suffering, the shrieks of the terror-stricken and the awful gasping of those in the last throes of drowning, none of us will ever forget to our dying day. . . ."

As the ship slipped downward, it broke in two pieces. The bow section (comprising three-fifths of the ship) descended downward, finally knifing its way 60 feet into the sediment at a 30-degree angle. The weight of the ship then broke it again so that it sat in an upright position on the bottom. The stern section, with its massive triple-expansion engines, followed minutes later, crashing onto the ocean floor. The force of the downblast (the water pressure following the ship created by its descent) finished the job. What remains today of the stern is a nearly unrecognizable mess 2,000 feet from the bow.

Debris from the now sunken ship floated everywhere, while a silent white iceberg with red paint smeared

A White Star brochure, featuring rates for first-class accommodations. The address at the bottom of the brochure's cover provided worried relatives and friends with a gathering place during the frantic few days after the sinking.
(SSHSA Collection, U of B Library)

on its base served as a reminder that the ship the newspapers once called "unsinkable" was gone forever.

At 4:10 a.m., the *Carpathia* arrived near the scene of the tragedy. Her captain and crew lent a helping hand to the weary survivors. Cold and hungry, the stunned passengers of the *Titanic* were offered food, blankets, and warm rooms. The *Carpathia* wasn't as luxurious as the *Titanic*, but no one thought to complain of the accommodations.

With an iceberg bearing a slight resemblance to the Rock of Gibraltar in the distance, the *Carpathia* abandoned her original plans and began a new voyage toward New York. When the count was taken aboard ship it was learned that 705 people had survived and 1,522 people had died.

Questions for Reflection

1. How many warnings did the *Titanic* receive before the tragedy occurred? Does God still send warnings to people?

2. Captain Smith ordered the lifeboats uncovered after the collision, but hesitated in ordering distress rockets to be fired. What rationalizations might Smith have entertained which prevented him from acting decisively?

3. Prior to the ship sailing, and during the voyage, there were no lifeboat drills. Why not?

4. The leader's example will eventually be imprinted upon the actions and lives of followers. What are ways a leader's philosophy affects the lives of followers?

Chapter 2

Iceberg - 1,
Titanic - 0

The train began slowing down and the now-familiar screech of brakes told me I had finally reached my destination: Belfast, Northern Ireland. Belfast is an attractive metropolis, not at all like one might imagine from all the publicity through the years. From the window seat I could see the enormous yellow H & W crane looming high above the shipyard dominating the landscape as far as the eye could see.

Making my way through the turnstile and out of the train station, I was hit in the face with a blustery, cold March wind. Reminding myself that the 30-minute walk would still be worth all my efforts, I zipped my spring jacket far enough up to pinch my neck, and headed off.

After checking with a security guard, I hastened my pace along the wide streets of the Harland and Wolff shipyard, looking at the old brick buildings. My goal was to "see" the *Titanic*. As a writer, I need to fully experience what I write about, so the opportunity to visit Belfast in 1993 was too tempting to resist.

Harland and Wolff doesn't make ocean liners anymore. Fierce competition and the obvious profits to be made in the lucrative oil business made constructing tankers a better way to go.

After talking to a half-dozen people, I finally arrived at the scene. No shrine or memorial welcomed me. An old, dilapidated dock, and a small, rusting gate were the only visible relics of a time when the *Titanic* was the pride of all the world. I wasn't completely disappointed, however. No one could reasonably expect a world-class shipyard to spend time and money preserving monuments to ships they built which have sunk!

Standing there, I could imagine what it must have been like. I could almost hear the colossal triple-expansion engines as the *Titanic* slowly steamed away from Belfast amidst the hundreds who came to cheer and wave. She must have been a proud sight to the thousands of men who had labored night and day to make her the greatest ship ever built.

It wouldn't take much imagination to envision the *Titanic* moving crisply through the waves of the Atlantic toward New York, her engines moving ever faster. A cold, moonless night. I can almost smell the gray, water-saturated icebergs. It is quiet — too quiet — as Fredrick Fleet faces forward, scanning the horizon from the crows' nest. Suddenly a blank look of terror moves across his face when Fred's deepest fears are realized. There is no turning back. . . .

There is almost a religious quality about this story.

The *Titanic* is a ship you do not easily walk away from. Other maritime tragedies have been buried in our memories and nearly forgotten altogether, but R.M.S. *Titanic* won't seem to go away. She has kept our interest for decades.

Admittedly, few events in history have arrested my attention with such intensity as the *Titanic*. To this day I am still awed by pictures of her. Reading over the events of that April night, an overwhelming sense of quietness and contemplation comes upon me. The *Titanic* is more than history — much more.

The *Titanic* disaster has prophetic significance, and understanding why is the quest of this book. I am convinced that Robert Ballard's discovery in 1985 was orchestrated by God for a unique objective. While men may toast their own genius and technical proficiency for the find, God, in His wisdom and for His purposes, kept the *Titanic* "lost" for 73 years.

Ballard himself — a professional explorer — could not escape the depth of emotional conflict that the *Titanic* birthed in his consciousness. Unregenerate men instinctively recognize there is something innately spiritual about this ship, but are not sure how to vent their feelings.

God is speaking directly to our society but more specifically, His church, through this mammoth hulk of rusted steel laying on the bottom of the Atlantic Ocean. The dynamics of her construction, the experiences of her crew, the events leading to her destruction, and the dramatic rescue of her survivors, all parallel Church conditions of today with astounding accuracy. This is not only the story of a shocking catastrophe. The *Titanic* and all of its intricacies embody a wake-up call to the body of Christ.

Getting Our Bearings

There were four ships who played significant parts in the unfolding of this drama: the *Titanic*, the *Californian*, the *Samson*, and the *Carpathia*. Each exemplifies for us a methodology of approach to Christian service.

I wish to make abundantly clear that my focus is upon groups that acknowledge Jesus Christ as Lord and the Bible as His legitimate Word. Other groups may meet in ornate buildings, but by biblical standards are no more New Testament churches than the local V.F.W. or Rotary Club. The Church is not an organization or a club, but a living organism, created by Christ to express His love and power to a needy world.

The sphere in which we will focus our attention then is made up of born-again, Bible-believing Christians. The Church consists of those who gather in His name. Whether they meet in or out of denominational walls is irrelevant.

I doubt many pastors or church members consider *Titanic*'s fate to be relevant to the problems they face in their local churches. What could an old ship have to say to the crises we face in this generation? A closer examination reveals, however, a frightening similarity between the leadership methods aboard the *Titanic* and those operating through many church systems today. My objective is not to discourage or condemn ministers or church leaders — I'm one myself. Rather, I would like us to perceive the selfish motives behind many of our methods that ultimately undermine our effectiveness. The goal of every Christian must be focused toward becoming the church Jesus died to create.

Philosophy of Ministry

The *Titanic*, like many churches, had its own unique system. A system is defined as: "a group of interacting, interrelated, or interdependent elements forming a complex whole." That is quite a mouthful, but essentially, people and things operating together begin to assume a particular identity.

A large insurance company, for example, has a system of operation. The elements of time, space, money, people, individual functions, facility, furniture, and parking are all interacting, interrelated and often interdependent elements, but come together to form the complex whole. The company is perceived by the population as one unit, even though these complexities exist. When you call up to acquire a policy, you do not think of all of their interrelating parts. You expect that they will get you what you need: insurance!

Behind that system of operation is a philosophy. The leadership, headed by the president, may be service-oriented, for example. Therefore, each department head will emphasize service and a caring concern for the customer. Employees will then find their "value" by how well they serve the customer. All activity and motivation in the company will be directly affected by this philosophy.

Captain Smith's philosophy of operation (which included his beliefs, attitudes, likes, and dislikes) strongly influenced every aspect of life aboard the *Titanic*, determining not only **what** but **how** daily decisions were made. Every department strove to come in line with their commander's philosophy. Consciously or unconsciously, Smith's way of doing things became the ship's standard operating procedure.

Churches have systems, and function according to particular philosophies as well. The leadership develops this philosophy on purpose or incidentally without the conscious awareness of anyone in the church. Either way, a philosophy of ministry exists, and each member conforms to it.

Every church system is driven by a philosophy of ministry. The values of the leader or leadership team leave their mark not only on **what** is done, but **how** it is done.

The philosophy of ministry determines how a given church will express their Christian beliefs in a locality. Declared rules and regulations together with unspoken or assumed rules and regulations will affect every aspect of church life.

For example, Rev. Johnston's sermon is briefly distracted one Sunday morning by the late arrival of the McKoys, a new family to the church. People turn around as they hear them file into the last pew. The looks on each face register a certain amount of disapproval, since none of the McKoy family are especially dressed up. The McKoys have encountered a church system and philosophy of ministry likely to drive them away. The unspoken rules and regulations are: 1) late arrival is always inexcusable, 2) the sermon is central to all church activity, and 3) no one is accepted without the proper attire.

The above is just a small example, but virtually every aspect of church life has its own system which is driven consciously or unconsciously by a philosophy of ministry shaped by leadership. This philosophy either enhances the church's effectiveness toward accomplishing its mission or nullifies its ability to bless anyone.

The *Titanic*, as a system, had a specific philosophy behind its everyday operation. Decisions were handed down by leadership according to specific values. These values included excellence, image, and profit. Nearly every leadership decision could find its root in one of these three underlying motivations.

Cunard had recently built the *Lusitania* and was working on the *Mauretania*. In those days, with emigrants streaming to the United States, passenger lines raced to gobble up the profits sure to come to those who provided the means of travel. Driven by the accomplishments of

Cunard, White Star strove to build greater and larger luxury liners.

Everything about the *Titanic* was the best. It might help us relate to her size if we thought of reaching the top of an 11-story building and looking down. That is how tall the *Titanic* was. She was the largest, most exquisite, most expensive ship afloat. Nothing in the mind and imagination of man had been withheld from her design. A true work of art in the shipbuilding industry, she was more elegant and more exciting than any other ship in existence.

Excellence excites the imagination and makes people feel special. We all appreciate a job done well — a project which performs better than expected or a meal cooked just right. Paul the Apostle urges Christians to strive for excellence in Colossians 3:23: "Whatever you do, work at it with all your heart, as working for the Lord, not for men."

The focus of excellence, however, is designed to bless our God, not impress our fellow man. The drive for excellence among the leadership and crew of the *Titanic* came from their second value: image. They wanted to appear the best, the richest, the strongest, the most superior ship in the world. Such an image made them feel secure about themselves. The crew became intoxicated with the image of success. But, in spite of her technology, size, prestige, and marketing, the *Titanic* was still, in essence, just a ship!

Sixteen watertight compartments supposedly made the *Titanic* unsinkable.[1] The engineers, proud of their accomplishment, carelessly spoke of the *Titanic* as being practically "unsinkable." The press picked up on the idea and spoonfed it to the public. "It was deadly presumption for the engineers to proclaim the ship unsinkable; this sowed the seeds of complacency in the leadership on the *Titanic* which was the single greatest reason for the disaster."[2]

When the *Titanic* was built, the welfare of each passenger was not the focus, though it appeared that way. The care taken to provide exquisite comfort created the image that the *Titanic* was designed for the benefit of others. She was not. The *Titanic* was built to satisfy the third value, financial profit to the company. Outwardly then, the *Titanic* conveyed the image of safety and luxury, when in reality she was an accident waiting to happen.

Standard procedure mandated that boat drills were to be held any Sunday morning the liner was at sea. The *Titanic* never held one.[3] Such drills seemed irrelevant to the captain and crew. This carelessness doomed more than 500 people unnecessarily. Critical minutes ticked by as crewman struggled to learn how to properly deploy the lifeboats. When the boats were ready for boarding, none of the crewmen knew how many passengers they could hold! Scores of families perished needlessly because the crew had not been trained properly.

Smith knew that April was the worst iceberg month. This was the time of year when rising temperatures broke them free from northern glaciers. He believed that his vast experience, coupled with this new technology, could mount any obstacle.

Seven-eighths of any iceberg is underwater. Most are 3,000 years old! The berg the *Titanic* hit weighed approximately one billion pounds — 10 times her own weight. Icebergs get harder with time, and hitting one is like ramming into a small island. In effect, the captain commanded his ship to steam full speed into a cluster of islands without the benefit of a map to reveal where he was going![4]

The philosophy of operation including excellence, image, and profit was rooted in self. Pride blinded the minds of nearly everyone onboard. God, in His mercy, sent the *Titanic* no less than six messages warning of impending disaster. In each case, and for various reasons, the captain and crew ignored those warnings to their own peril.

Many Evangelical churches throughout America have lost touch with their mission and are speeding toward destruction with the same blind pridefulness. We have become polarized; transfixed upon methodologies that God used years ago, never grasping that it was the Spirit of God in those methods which brought blessing and revival.

Far too many expressions of the local church are centered on their own organization, or worse, around the pastor who drives it. The purpose of people coming together as a church body has lost its meaning. Many Christians gather on Sunday mornings out of habit or a sense of obligation, not to fellowship with the Body and hear from heaven.

Consider the typical church with its many programs and traditions. Is it truly vital for members to attend week in and week out? Are leaders indisputably focused upon serving each member, or feeling good about themselves because the pews are filled? Do we want to help people discover their spiritual gifts or do we want them to come so their tithe can help pay salaries? Is it a caring ministry we seek to build, or a well-oiled ministry machine?

In pastor-centered churches, (PCC) most activity is designed to perpetuate the leader's ministry. He is the gifted man. His preaching is what matters. Individual members growing in their spiritual gifts and callings is a nice concept, but seldom, if ever, occurs. When any one individual becomes overly enthusiastic about God, the PCC ships them to Bible school so they can develop their own PCC.

Captain Edward Smith was like so many church leaders today: polished, experienced, well-liked — but careless. Successful church leaders can easily be promoted to god-like status. If they actually believe half of the accolades, they become targets of deception for the devil who knows how to trap men with pride. No matter how "high" we get, our greatest call remains servanthood.

Past laurels give us praise among men, but can disqualify us from God's purposes now. David maintained a life of balance, proclaiming: "I would rather be a doorkeeper in the house of my God than dwell in the tents of the wicked" (Ps. 84:10). Though he had much to boast of as king over Israel, he fully realized that his victories were all God's doing.

When churches do not make disciple-making their central focus, crisis eventually destroys them. We believe we are making disciples with our emphasis on Bible exposition each Sunday morning, but if that is so, where are they? Have our congregations learned anything? You bet they have! They have learned that disciples are faithful church attenders who listen to pastors preach, but are not changing and applying God's Word to their everyday lives. Making New Testament disciples has little or nothing to do with attending Sunday or midweek services.

The Jesus method for making disciples involved spending discretionary time with them. Followers became disciples as they experienced the full range of Jesus' ministry. They ate together, hung out together, laughed and cried together, and experienced persecution together. Jesus was not stingy with delegating responsibility, either. He sent them out to minister without a bachelor's degree and without training them in proper biblical exegesis. Remember, Judas was included among those who healed the sick and cast demons out of people.

Throughout my years of pastoral ministry, I have been privileged to examine every major doctrine of Scripture. Key verses have been extrapolated, expounded upon, and delivered with passion to the congregations I have served. Never have I witnessed men or women become disciples through hearing my sermons alone. Yet, the Great Commission of Jesus Christ is: "Go and . . . make disciples of all nations" (Matt. 28:18). We have produced attenders, but not disciples.

When Image Collides with Reality

"Many were not informed of the seriousness of the damage: both they and the passengers were left to speculate as to what was happening."[5] One steward told a passenger, "There is talk of an iceberg, ma'am, and they have stopped not to run into it."[6]

"Firemen William Nutbean and John Podesta couldn't get shipmates to stir from their bunks. The men were taking the news of the iceberg as a joke. Then fireman Eustace Blann appeared holding a lump of ice. 'Look what I found on deck!' he cried, his face pale and lips quivering. A moment later boatman Alfred Nichols came to the door shouting, 'Get your lifebelts and man your boats!' "[7]

Confusion abounded aboard the doomed ship until moments before the *Titanic* slipped beneath the waves.

Conflicting orders were passed to passengers. One moment they would be told to prepare to abandon ship; another, they would be told to go back to their cabins because there was no danger whatsoever.

This condition aboard ship directly parallels many churches. Since disciple-making and leadership development are not the central focus, individuals are granted titles based on faithfulness to the church. However, they are never trained to lead! They know how to obey the pastor, but not how to discern for themselves what God is saying. When crises come (and they always do), pastor-dependent followers are incapable of providing leadership. The congregations they serve become confused, not knowing who to trust.

Contrast this condition with the counsel Paul gave Timothy: "And the things you have heard me say in the presence of many witnesses entrust to reliable men who will also be qualified to teach others" (2 Tim. 2:2). Paul was not raising up automatons. The purpose of other believers was not to use them. Paul discipled Timothy to utilize his own spiritual gifts to better the Church. Timothy was to disciple others, not by producing cookie-cutter copies of himself, but by helping them discover their gifts and callings and then training them in character development.

Consider the number of churches which fall apart when the pastor transfers, dies, or quits. Elders and deacons have not been trained to lead, but to follow. The *Titanic* warns us of a leadership style designed to convey an image instead of empowering disciples. We're not called to preach magnificent sermons. We're called to produce magnificent disciples.

Communication

Making disciples involves time and communication. The communication on the *Titanic* was astoundingly poor. Why? Following orders was viewed as more important than understanding orders. No one asked questions. As a result, bad choices became fatal choices.

Consider for a moment the wireless operators. Wireless was essentially a new phenomenon. The operators were not crew members but employees of the Marconi Company. Nevertheless, their purpose was to serve the interests of the crew and passengers of the ship. They also had the responsibility to report to the bridge any message concerning navigation. But, the procedures affecting communication between the bridge and the wireless room were almost nonexistent.

The wireless operators represented the *Titanic*'s ability to "listen" to others. Beginning Sunday afternoon, reports began reaching them of icebergs ahead. Each warning had interesting dynamics attached to it.

The first warning (from the *Caronia*) should have arrested the leadership's attention. After all, *Rappahannock*'s eyewitness experience of icebergs the night before made this first wireless warning all the more ominous. The plan to impress the New York crowd with the *Titanic*'s speed and prowess should have been scrapped. The first priority needed to shift from speed to protecting lives. Though the message was posted for the officers to see, no order was given to slow down.

The second message (from the *Baltic*) was given to the captain as he ate lunch with Bruce Ismay. Not only did it warn of ice fields, but it also conveyed a distress call: "Last night we spoke with German oil tanker *Deutschland*, Stettin to Philadelphia, not under control;

short of coal; latitude 40.42 north, longitude 55.11. Wishes to be reported to New York and other steamers." The captain did not seem to care. He handed it to Ismay without comment, who promptly put it in his pocket. Later that afternoon, Ismay conversed with a passenger:

"We are in among the icebergs," Ismay announced cavalierly, fishing the *Baltic*'s telegram out of his pocket and holding it out for Mrs. Ryerson to see. She glanced at it, noticing the mention of the tanker *Deutschland*. "We are not going very fast, 20 or 21 knots," he continued, "but we are going to start up some new boilers this evening."

"What is the rest of the telegram?" Mrs. Ryerson asked.

"It is the *Deutschland* wanting a tow, not under control," he replied.

"What are you going to do about that?"

Ismay replied that they were not going to do anything about the *Deutschland*, but would instead reach New York early and surprise everyone. He wanted to show just what the *Titanic* could do.[8]

Ismay expressed a lot in this conversation. As managing director, image was his most important concern. Helping other ships in trouble was secondary. This was in keeping with the philosophy of the *Titanic*. There is a trace of racism involved here as well, for the British disliked the Germans (remember, they would be enemies on the battlefield in three more years). They wouldn't think of changing course to offer assistance to **Germans**. From a communications standpoint, their enemy was asking for mercy, but the *Titanic* was too engulfed in its own selfishness to consider the needs of others. No efforts were made to help at all. Sound familiar?

The third message never reached Smith. No one wanted to bother the captain while he ate. Why? What prevents people from inconveniencing leadership with bad news? Pastor-controlled churches create an aura of fear around leadership. Fear prevents church members from speaking up about things that need change. The similarities here are astounding.

Message number four was ignored by the wireless operators. Overworked and distracted by circumstances beyond their control, the strongest warning yet was put aside and never delivered to the bridge.

The final warning from the *Californian* was greeted with the words, "shut up" from the wireless operator. He had *more important* things to do. What things? Seeing to it that the paying passengers got a chance to send meaningless greetings to family and friends with this new toy. He had no time to communicate with *inferior* ships, anyway. What could they say which could possibly have significance to the invincible *Titanic*?

While it may seem like a terrible thing to suggest at this point, could it be that God himself sunk the *Titanic*? When we examine the facts, no other conclusion seems possible:

Weather: The night was crisp and clear, but moonless, reducing visibility.

Sea Conditions: The smoothest Second Officer Lightoller had ever seen in his career. The water was like a sea of glass. Sighting icebergs at night depended upon the ocean lapping up against the base of the berg. The still water kept lookouts from spotting it in time.

Timing: Had the *Titanic* left an hour later, or been delayed through a variety of mishaps that nearly kept her from leaving, no accident would have occurred. In addition, God could have influenced the wind and waves to prevent the iceberg from being where it was at that moment.

The Iceberg: It traveled for two years to arrive at the spot where the tragedy occurred. In addition, bergs turn over in the water from time to time. Lightoller believed that the berg the *Titanic* hit had recently turned over in the water. As a result, it might have been a water-saturated, blue-gray color instead of white, making it that much more difficult to identify.

Why would a loving God send 1,522 innocent men, women, and children to their deaths? How could a God of justice be so cruel? This appears to be a facet of God's nature that we are terrified to consider. And, while we might blithely stutter, "It's a mystery we won't understand this side of heaven," I believe the answer may be nearer than we perceive.

First, we humans place the highest premium on this life. To us, our life on this planet is everything. To God, it is a drop in the bucket of eternity. God, as sovereign Lord, reserves the right to do with His creation as He purposes for reasons of greater eternal weight than we can imagine (Rom. 9:21, 11:22; 2 Tim. 2:20-21). We need to remember, especially in this multi-cultural, independence-worshipping society, that we are the created. He is the Creator.

Secondly, with this mindset firmly established, we can gain wisdom from God as to His heart during this disaster. One might easily say that God passively allowed hundreds to drown and freeze to death. But, was God passive?

I believe that God fully desired to save the *Titanic*

from its fate. Remember, it was God in His mercy who sent six specific warnings to the crew via other ships. He wanted to save them from destruction, but pridefulness blinded their eyes and stopped their ears from discerning the danger they were in.

There is a place in God when He will not cross the line of our free will, even if it means our destruction. This not only applies to the *Titanic*, but to churches as well.

Church leaders: Are you able to hear the voice of the Lord? If you are, consider yourself among the few. Hundreds of churches across the country remain self-absorbed, blinded with ambition to be the biggest and the greatest. God, in His mercy, sends warnings — usually by people or leaders we consider to be inferior to ourselves. If we humble ourselves and listen, God can save us. If, in our pridefulness, we continue on with our programs and arrogant ambitions, not even God can rescue us.

The lack of communication was not only external to other ships, but internal among crew members. George Rowe did not even know there was a collision until one hour after the event. If he had not seen a lifeboat in the water and called the bridge, he might never have known. From the top down, no one was passing along vital information.

Communication in PCC churches follows the same patterns. Since power is often closely linked to possessing information, those in leadership are threatened by the prospect of sharing it. Relationships are built around retaining power rather than helping the church function. In times of crisis, such churches become rumor mills as members gossip, reason, and speculate how to solve problems. Confusion destroys more lives than the church crisis itself.

Reflection or Deflection?

The *Titanic* is a study in the variety of ways in which pride ultimately destroys an organization. Pride appears harmless (even considered a virtue by some), yet is the chief reason many local churches go out of business shortly after looking like they would set the world on fire. Pride was the sin which felled the greatest of all angels, and it is the tool that angel now uses to bring ruin to churches of many sizes, shapes, and colors.

Pride is deceitful. No one thinks they have it! Prideful people look upon others as the cause for their difficulties, never perceiving that they might originate with themselves. Pride is therefore deflective, pointing the finger away from itself as the culprit for failure.

Some years ago, I attended a ministers' seminar. There, a nationally-recognized author and teacher shared his perceptions of the sort of fig leaves clergy tend to wear. The accuracy of each sentence pierced through my heart as the message laid bare internal attitudes I harbored directly opposite of biblical standards.

At the conclusion of his message, the speaker allowed time for questions and comments. I was speechless. I knew he had spoken a prophetic message that applied to every one of us. Through God's Spirit, he had punched the lights out of our religious facades.

I paused to listen. The only question I thought appropriate would be, "Where can we get a good bargain on sackcloth and ashes in this town?" That is not what I heard. Instead of groans of repentance, I endured a favorite ministerial pastime: deflection.

Deflection occurs when individuals shield themselves from the conviction of God's Word to hide their own sins. Some examples of deflections I heard that morning included:

"Brother, the word you shared was good. I wish other ministers I know were here to experience it. They needed it." (Translation: I certainly don't need this teaching, they do!)

"I am so excited about what you are sharing. This confirms what we have been doing in our church for the last six months!" (Translation: In reality, this statement was not only awfully close to lying, but the teaching had his name in red written all over it.)

"Isn't it great when God speaks to us? We're glad this brother is here to share . . . blah, blah, blah. (Translation: Maybe if I compliment the speaker long enough, it will appear that the message wasn't aimed at me.)

Messages from God cut through our facades, challenging the mindsets we so confidently trust in. God used this servant of the Lord to call for repentance and attitudinal change. The primary purpose of the Holy Spirit in coming to us is to convict of sin, righteousness, and judgment (John 16:8). When we deflect, we give lip-service to God's words, pretending we are in complete agreement.

In effect, I affirm that the message preached was true but take no steps to change my behavior. Deflection is a socially acceptable form of self-deception that helps people escape repentance. It was just this form of pride that ultimately destroyed the *Titanic*, and it continues to do the same to churches throughout the land.

Any human method we use to deflect God's words to us will be judged. Several of the churches represented at that seminar I mentioned experienced dramatic splits and loss of attendance within three years. No matter how we choose to define it, turning a deaf ear to God's Spirit invites God's wrath. Our reputations hold no weight in heaven.

Change or Sink

The *Titanic* wasn't just a ship, she was an outlook on life. If she was merely steel and wood, fascination surrounding her would have perished along with her years ago. This ship encompasses a great deal more than the sum of its parts. The *Titanic* lays in two gigantic pieces on the ocean floor as a memorial, displaying for us a philosophy born of pride.

The only way for the Church today to escape certain destruction is through humility of mind and a servant's heart among the leadership. You may value excellence, and attempt to polish an image of respectability, but God views such as dung in his sight. Whatever the Lord has blessed our individual churches with is never meant to hoard and immortalize through monuments of wood and stone. The resources He entrusts us with are to bless His body.

For far too long we ministers have given lip service to the concept that "we are all the body of Christ." How many of us truly hurt when other churches are hurting or care about the body of Christ in our city? It is time to put away the rhetoric, and begin serving each other in concrete ways.

Questions for Reflection

1. The builders of the *Titanic* wanted her to appear to be the best ship in the world. How does this parallel today's Church?

2. No expense was spared to craft an image of success for the *Titanic,* yet the original plans calling for up to 48 lifeboats was scuttled to keep the costs down. How does this attitude apply to the Church today?

3. Leaders can easily be promoted to "god-like" status through polished preaching or successful programs. How can pastors de-emphasize themselves and strengthen the Church to accomplish its mission?

4. What are some of the reasons communication was so poor aboard the *Titanic?* What applications might these have to the Church?

5. What might be one reason the *Titanic* failed to listen to warnings? Why do *Titanic* churches ignore the counsel of other churches?

The *Titanic*'s crow's nest, from which lookout Frederick
Fleet spotted the iceberg 37 seconds before the collision.
Fleet rang the bell, then phoned down to the bridge.
(Courtesy of Ken Marschall)

Chapter 3

Escape from the *Titanic*!

Few people thought the curious scraping noise they heard in the middle of the night was particularly serious. Some thought a propeller blade had broken off; others thought the anchor chain was being let out; still others, that pillow fights were in progress in adjoining rooms.

Accompanying the sudden noise was an eerie quiet. The familiar hum of the engines had ceased, and it felt like the *Titanic* had slowed down. Nevertheless, passengers were inclined to trust the leadership and accept the explanations some crew members offered, regardless of how contradictory they were.

Twenty minutes following the accident, Captain Smith received the assessment from Fourth Officer Boxhall: water was flowing into five, perhaps six compartments of the ship. The *Titanic* had been designed to withstand the breaching of four compartments without difficulty. The number of compartments breached meant the ship would not survive.

As chief executive officer, the captain knew the awful truth: Hundreds of people would die within a few short hours. He would not leisurely retire, living out the rest of his days as an honored officer. Instead, he would be buried alive at sea — and many others would join him.

With the crisis now upon him, it was time for action, but Smith acted neither swiftly nor decisively. Eyewitnesses described his face as dazed during much of the ordeal. Some have reasoned that he was deliberately avoiding panic. Others have advanced the unlikely theory that he was in a stupor from too many drinks that night. Whatever the case, the captain was faced with a mind-numbing dilemma: Who would be allowed to live and who would be left to die?

Smith's first command, 25 minutes following the collision, was to ready the lifeboats. Loaded to capacity, they would still not be able to save half of the passengers aboard. In addition, none of the crew had yet participated in a proper lifeboat drill!

Minutes ticked by, yet no general alarm was raised or distress rockets fired. Though some crew members had received the order to prepare lifeboats for launching, many others had not. "A clear breakdown in the lines of shipboard communication had taken place, a breakdown that would not improve as the crew continued to sink and the slope of the ship became alarming."[1] The lights still shone brightly, while the band continued to play ragtime.

From a distance, the *Titanic* looked like the perfect postcard, all lit up on a clear, calm night. Many crewmen reinforced the false sense of security, either intentionally or because they themselves couldn't believe the ship was sinking fast.[2]

" 'Lifeboats!' one woman cried out. 'What do they need of lifeboats? This ship could smash a hundred icebergs and not feel it. Ridiculous!' "[3] Denial grew and prevailed for some time among the passengers and crew. This mindset undoubtedly caused many more unnecessary deaths. Since nearly everyone strongly believed the *Titanic* was invincible, they were unable to perceive reality as it unfolded.

Adding to this condition, a number of crewmen were preventing passengers from leaving third-class compartments. The gates leading from the well deck had been locked.[4] Whether accidentally or on purpose, first and second-class passengers were being provided the first opportunity to escape.

"Ladies, this way," First Officer Murdoch called to a small crowd of passengers. There was no response. No one wanted to leave the apparent safety of the solid *Titanic* for a tiny, frail boat on the North Atlantic.[5] Finally, passengers were prevailed upon to appear on deck with life preservers, having received instructions from various stewards. The first passengers were loaded into lifeboat #7 and lowered at 12:25 a.m., or 45 minutes after the collision took place.

Fourth Officer Joseph Boxhall remained at the wheel, even when he knew the *Titanic* would go no further. Quartermaster George Rowe had been doing his duty as well, keeping watch at the stern of the ship. He saw what appeared to be a lifeboat in the water and called the bridge. Rowe was ordered to bring signaling devices at once so that other ships could be alerted.

White rockets burst into a fireworks display high above the *Titanic* — always a distress signal at sea. Every five to six minutes they went off, and before the night was over, at least eight were sighted by the *Californian*, a ship in the immediate area.

Many of the lifeboats leaving the *Titanic* were only partially filled. Several passengers still refused to leave the warmth of the ship. They just did not believe it was really sinking. By the time it became obvious to the majority of passengers that the *Titanic* was sinking, most of the lifeboats were gone.[6] Officers were unfamiliar with the specially designed Welin davits, capable of carrying tremendous weight. They had never before conceived of the possibility of ever using davits to lower lifeboats. Stuck within this mindset, crewmen lowered many lifeboats with far less people on board than the 65 capacity. One lifeboat descended to the water below with only a dozen passengers. By the end of the evening the average would come to 44.

Thomas Andrews, managing director of Harland and Wolff, knew the lifeboats could hold more people. He had personally overseen the construction of the ship from the keel up. Fear and shock so paralyzed the normal thinking processes of men like him, that they were incapable of offering vital assistance during this time of crisis, other than urging some to put on lifebelts.

There were other problems — even among those fortunate enough to find a place aboard one of the lifeboats. Fifth Officer Lowe later reported: "Not every seaman member of a liner's crew was competent to handle a 30-foot lifeboat, or had even set foot in one. All-around seamen were rare aboard the *Titanic*. Many of the sailors could not row."[7] On lifeboat #3 the crewman at the tiller was so inexperienced he soon had the boat heading back to the sinking liner.[8]

Lawrence Beesley, himself a passenger aboard lifeboat #13 later testified: "I do not think they (crew) could have had any practice in rowing, for all night long their oars crossed and clashed; if our safety had depended on speed or accuracy in keeping time it would have gone hard with us. Shouting began from one end of the boat to the other as to what we should do, where we should go, and no one seemed to have any knowledge how to act. At last we asked, 'Who is in charge of this boat?' but there was no reply."[9]

During the subsequent investigation, and under interrogation by Senator Smith, Mrs. J. Stuart White testified: "The women did the rowing. Some of the men smoked their pipes, threatening each other and fighting." Lifeboat #8 carried just 28 people, though each lifeboat could hold nearly three times that number. The ship sloped downward while both the captain and Lightoller refused to break the rule: Women and children first, though only husbands remained in plain sight. Once aboard #8, the Countess of Rothes eventually took command of the tiller due to the incompetence of the assigned crewman. They spent a good part of the evening rowing toward a mysterious light in the distance, believed to be a tramp steamer, which they thought would most certainly rescue them.[10]

Five lifeboats now floated on the water and several others were in the process of being loaded. Still, few passengers had yet grasped the desperateness of their situation. Rumors of rescue by the ship in the distance or the *Titanic*'s sister ship, *Olympic,* kept everyone from fully realizing the danger they were in.

As the *Titanic* began to list, reality set in. Anxious fear evolved into panic as lifeboats continued to disappear from the deck. Officers assigned to the lifeboats were forced to use guns to keep men from taking a seat aboard lifeboats where the priority was women and children first.

Captain Smith used a megaphone to call several lifeboats back to pick up more passengers. All refused, fearing they would be swamped.

As the ship's bow continued to sink, and with all of the lifeboats gone, passengers vainly scrambled for higher ground toward the stern of the ship. Finally, the inevitable happened, and the *Titanic* descended in two massive pieces to the ocean floor.

A number of persistent rumors survive the sinking. One is that First Officer Murdock shot himself during the final moments before the *Titanic* went under.[11] Another is that Captain Smith dived into the ocean just as the ship sank and swam to overturned lifeboat collapsible B, where he was turned away for lack of room. Unproven stories like these have done much to keep fascination about the *Titanic* alive after more than eight decades.

John Jacob Astor, a famous millionaire, died when one of the smokestacks fell on him.[12] Evidently the tragedy of the *Titanic* made no class distinctions. His wife Madeline, pregnant with the couple's first child, survived in lifeboat #4.

With the ship out of sight, the panic, fear, and tension was far from over. Hundreds of people screamed for help in the frigid waters of the Atlantic. Few in the lifeboats, however, were moved to help the hundreds dying in the water. Most feared they would be swamped by rowing into such a throng of terrified victims.

A survivor, Jack Thayer (who was 17 at the time), later reported, "The partially filled lifeboats standing by, only a few hundred yards away, never came back. Why on earth they did not come back is a mystery. How could any human being fail to heed those cries. The most heartrending part of the whole tragedy was the failure, right after the *Titanic* sank, of those boats which were only partially loaded, to pick up the poor souls in the water. There they were, only four or five hundred yards away, listening to the cries, and still they did not come back. If they had turned back, several more hundred would have been saved. No one can explain it. It was not satisfactorily explained in any investigation."[13] Some of the pas-

A lined, cork life vest retrieved from the disaster site. The vest was taken from the body of a victim brought to Halifax, Nova Scotia, for burial. A total of 306 bodies were recovered, leaving 1,200 unaccounted for.
(Courtesy of the Mariner's Museum, Newport News, Virginia)

sengers of the lifeboats urged an attempt at rescuing survivors. In #8, the Countess of Rothes and several others wanted to return, but were overruled by the majority. In others, overbearing crewmen refused the counsel of many, successfully convincing those aboard that the drowning people would capsize their boat.

In boat after boat the story was the same: a timid suggestion, a stronger refusal, nothing done. Of 1,600 people who went down on the *Titanic,* only 13 were picked up by the 18 boats that hovered nearby. Boat D hauled in Mr. William Hoyt who died a few hours later. Boat 4 rescued five — not because it rowed back but because they were within reach. Only No. 14 returned to the scene.[14]

One story deserves mention, as told by Captain Arthur Rostron of the *Carpathia:*

> Some of the first boats may have got away not filled to capacity, but later others certainly were overloaded and there were heart-rending moments when too-well-laden boats pulling about encountered poor fellows swimming in that ice-cold sea.
>
> In this case I am recounting a boat's gunwale (the upper edge of a ship's side) was seized forward by a swimmer. It was well before dawn. No one could see who it was, but many voices were raised protesting against him being hauled in.
>
> "We are full; we are full," they cried. "Don't let him come in!"
>
> One woman in the stern sheets, however, nursing her sorrow of a husband left behind on

the sunken ship, begged for the swimmer to be taken in. The pity in her pleading prevailed and she knew the swimmer had been saved before she sank back into the frozen coma that great tragedy engenders.

Hours passed. At length dawn lit the haggard faces of those who huddled shiveringly in that boat. Only then did the woman see the features of the drenched man she had been chiefly instrumental in dragging from a death by drowning.

It was her own husband.[15]

The passengers of the other lifeboats, however, were far too self-preoccupied to risk taking on those needing assistance regardless of the cries for help. Most remained paralyzed by the fear they would be swamped, and so did nothing.

As those in the boats listened, the sounds of the people struggling in the ocean gradually died away until, around 3:00 a.m., 40 minutes after the *Titanic* had sunk, they ceased.[16] For more than one hour, the survivors did all they could to cope with the icy cold air and water. Several of the lifeboats tied up to each other to become a mini-flotilla. They talked openly of their chances for survival. Many gave up hope. Others firmly believed they would be imminently saved. Some, overcome by the cold, died and were cast back into the ocean. As it turned out, the idealists would win out. A little after 4:00 a.m., the *Carpathia* was sighted coming their way.

The British inquiry into the events surrounding the tragedy tended to whitewash the whole affair. The aim seemed to lean toward exonerating White Star from blame while scapegoating another ship nearby which apparently did nothing to help. However, the British were not the only people with an interest in the *Titanic*.

When the U.S. Senate inquiry concluded its investigation they reached their own conclusions:

- Captain Smith's indifference to danger was a direct cause of the disaster: he was over-confident.
- The organization of the escape was haphazard.
- A higher proportion of third-class passengers was lost because they were given no warning before the ship was doomed.
- Some lifeboats were only partially loaded; none had compasses and only three had lamps. They were so badly manned that if their rescue had been delayed they would have been crushed by the advancing ice flow, "nearly 30 miles in width and rising 16 feet above the sur-

Titanic survivors as photographed from the deck of the *Carpathia.* *(Courtesy of Grant Freeman)*

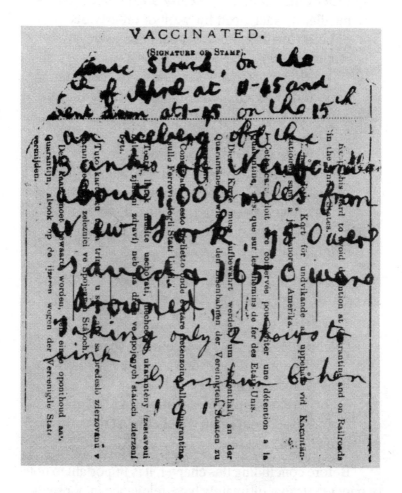

A hastily-written account of the sinking, from the
vaccination card of third-class passenger Gurshon "Gus"
Cohen. It reads: "*Titanic* struck, on the 14th of April at
11:45 and went down at 1:45 on the 15th an iceberg off
the Banks of Newfoundland about 1,000 miles from
New York. 750 were saved & 1650 were drowned.
Taking only 2 hours to sink. Gurshon Cohen, 1912."
(SSHSA Collection, U of B Library)

face of the water. . . ." Nearly 500 people were needlessly sacrificed for want of orderly discipline in loading the few boats that were provided.

• Some crew never reported to their stations and deserted their ship too quickly. Some were shockingly indifferent to the plight of others, remaining at a safe distance in partially-filled boats while others drowned.

• The use of wireless at sea must be reformed. Wages should go up, to discourage operators from exploiting tragedies.

• Wireless apparatus should be manned night and day.[17]

In addition, the inquiry, led by Senator Smith, made several recommendations. Among them:

• All passenger ships must carry lifeboats able to accommodate everyone on board.

• Regular lifeboat drills must be held utilizing the crews assigned to them.

• Steamships must carry searchlights. Twenty-four hour radio watches must be maintained on all vessels.[18]

Before concluding this chapter, it is important to note two incidents that ultimately have relevance in our search for the prophetic meaning of the *Titanic*'s disaster.

First, some believe the lifeboats were not disposed of after the *Titanic* went down. After they were returned to New York with the *Carpathia*, White Star removed their company flags and nameplates. Since the lifeboats were in good shape, it is likely they were transferred to other ships. After all, they had only been used once![19]

Secondly, it is interesting to note the treatment afforded the families of deceased band members. Under special arrangements with White Star, they went aboard as second-class passengers. White Star hired them through the Black family talent agency, who in turn paid them disgraceful wages. Not only did White Star and the agency refuse to compensate these unfortunate families in any way, but the Black agency actually billed them for the lost uniforms![20] While front page news coverage heralded the band members as heroes, White Star and the Blacks ignored the cries for help coming from the wives and children.

A lifeboat drill on the *Olympic* — made necessary by the events of April 14-15. *(Courtesy of Ken Marschall)*

⟩

Titanic's lifeboats in New York. The men pictured here give a good indication of the size of each boat; up to 65 passengers could safely occupy a lifeboat, but several leaving the *Titanic* carried only a handful. *(Courtesy of Ken Marschall)*

Questions for Reflection

1. Crewmen on the *Titanic*'s lifeboats were virtually helpless when it came to navigation on the open ocean. Why do you think crewmen were so incompetent?

2. Dozens of people died in the freezing water after the *Titanic* sank, because those in the lifeboats refused to go back. Is there a spirit of sacrifice and help in your church when brethren are hurting?

3. The horror of the sinking made no class distinctions; the rich died with the poor. Do we as humans have the power to elude judgment indefinitely? How does God's timetable for justice differ from our own?

4. Even after the encounter with the iceberg, passengers failed to see the danger. Why? How did leadership help to keep denial alive?

5. Fourth Officer Joseph Boxhall remained at the wheel even after the collision, when he knew the ship was stopped. Can you think of instances where leadership insists on keeping the appearance that all is well . . . when it is not?

Chapter 4

The Plumb Line

The voyage of the *Titanic* offers us a unique look into what happens to church systems and philosophies after leaders are gone. Captain Smith was no longer giving orders. The First Church of the *Titanic* was closed indefinitely with little hope of reopening. What would those left behind do? Would their lives imitate Christ? Would all men know they were His disciples by their love?

The proof of any pudding is in the eating. The validity of a philosophy of ministry or the correctness of a church system is proven by the quality of people it leaves behind.

As we have had opportunity to see, the philosophy of ministry aboard the *Titanic* was built around excellence, image, and profit. Communication came from the top down. Serving and modeling from those with titles was almost nonexistent.

Most of us are familiar with the movie, *It's a Wonderful Life,* starring James Stewart. This Frank Capra classic gets more air time than any other movie around the holiday season. The film is about a man who struggles his way through life, never getting a shot at his dreams. Eventually, he decides to commit suicide, believing that his existence was meaningless. An angel grants him a wish in the process — that the world would function as if he had never been born — and he is then introduced to the condition of his hometown without George Bailey.

Astonished at the crime, corruption, and unrest he witnesses, George eventually discovers that his life did have meaning because he valued people. Those he valued in turn cared for others creating a community built upon mutual support. Through the angel's good grace, he was permitted to return to his struggling life where he instantly appreciated every person and circumstance.

George learned something vital that Christians need to discover: Our lives have value to the degree we care for and live to bless others. Leaders are set in the body by God to provide role models of caring. We are not only called upon to "preach the word," but call men to "imitate (us) as we imitate Christ." Therefore, to the degree our philosophies of ministry imitate Jesus, people will either begin to live and act like the Master or live and act like the selfish, prideful, apathetic believers we have become accustomed to in our churches.

How often I have heard pastors decry the attitudes and actions of their flocks while they model lives that are exactly the same! Our church members often only mimic the attitudes they see lived out through their leadership.

The events which unfolded during the few minutes passengers spent aboard the lifeboats were a real-life test of the philosophy of operation aboard the *Titanic*. Just like any church, the measure of success is determined by how people act when out from under the watchful eye of human authority.

Trust Me!

Passengers and crew alike were confident their ship was invincible. This attitude mirrors how church members across our land feel about their institutions. Longevity ("Established since 3000 B.C."), size ("We run 32,000 in Sunday school every week"), money ("Our building is bought and paid for"), and recent history ("Last year two million people came to our services"), all lead the average Christian to a false sense of security surrounding his or her individual church. These conditions seem to naturally suggest God's unconditional favor. Maybe. Maybe not.

God's current blessings are not based on longevity, size, money, or recent history. Church systems and the philosophies that drive them have value to God only if they enable people to become more like Jesus. When Christians trust these carnal exterior conditions to be the measure of God's approval, they put their own spiritual lives at risk.

People aboard the *Titanic* developed their own ideas of what the curious noise was. Few people asked questions. They were intimidated by the awesomeness of the ship and judged themselves unwise to raise any concerns, yet questions might have saved many more people.

The lifeboats aboard the *Titanic* spiritually represented her ability to reach out to a lost and dying world. The *Titanic* did not train others to use lifeboats because the leadership considered the *Titanic* one giant lifeboat.

This attitude reflects the frame of mind many Evangelical churches exhibit throughout this country. There exists a subtle but very deliberate belief that our programs or services are the primary means through which salvation occurs. We plan activities to get people to our church buildings where they can be converted. We expect the lost to come to our services, our picnics, and our special events. If non-Christians are fortunate enough to find their way into the church building, fine. If not — too bad!

There were no lifeboat drills, just as there is little to no training for Christians in many churches toward reaching the lost. Believers are expected to bring the lost to the building, not win them to Christ themselves. The mentality is "come to us and be saved." It sounds much like the *Titanic*: "We don't need lifeboats — we are a lifeboat!" How absurd.

God is calling the church of Jesus Christ to be an army of rescuers. The structure never saves. It is a means to a destination, not the destination itself. Lifeboats symbolize the ways we as individual churches actively reach outside our comfort zones to touch those in need.

How drastically different our methods are to those of Jesus of Nazareth. We never read of Him inviting anyone to synagogue. He spent His time with people in their homes, their jobs, and their marketplaces. His energies were spent drawing men, women, and children to himself and training others to do the same. Today's Christians have been lured into accepting the Christian call to evangelize as a spectator sport, rather than signing on as participants.

Captain Smith spent the evening in a daze, like many of today's church leaders. Smith didn't consider failure as a possible outcome. As never before, he needed to be sharp, but the horror of the moment hindered timely decision-making.

Many of the *Titanic*'s passengers reacted to the news of a collision with total denial. I am always amazed when members play the denial game. The future of the Church teeters on the brink of collapse, yet they continue playing the songs (much like the band did). Why do Christians choose to preserve the image of safety while destruction is imminent?

I have talked to different church members through the years about potentially destructive patterns that visibly existed in their churches. I have asked about financial accountability or the depth of relationships among the leadership. Parishioners often use standard denial techniques. "Everything is okay. You're making something out of nothing." How sad to see them months later, disillusioned and determined never to be part of a church again.

Persuading people to accept reality is not easy. Each of us eventually reaches a point when we accept that problems do exist, but timing, as they say, is everything. Once the lifeboats were gone, the chance of survival severely decreased.

Having served aboard a *Titanic* church, it is easy now to look back and remember the people who tried to warn me that things were not right. With shame I recall laughing with other brothers of the preposterousness of their claims. (But they were right!) Those who warned me jumped aboard lifeboats to get away in time. Imagine my surprise when the ship began to go under at great speed with me still in leadership!

Success Without a Successor

For the 705 people fortunate to find their ways to lifeboats, the *Titanic* ordeal was far from over. Within moments of touching the waters of the Atlantic, no one had occasion to breathe a little easier.

As we have learned, most of the *Titanic*'s crew had received no training in the deploying or operation of lifeboats. In one instance, a professional yachtsman was called upon to help provide seamanship skills since those with a title were so inexperienced. On lifeboat #8 the ineptitude of crewmen aboard would become so great during the night that the women literally took command.

As we've seen, confusion reigned as oars clashed in the midst of heated arguments about the direction each boat would go. The boats themselves were committed to the ocean with many important survival items missing. They were thoroughly unprepared for this change of plans.

A friend of mine once said, "A success without a successor is a failure." The true measure of our leadership is the people we leave behind. The fruit of our ministry is not programs, buildings, or church attendance lists that are all continually fluctuating. Fruit can be measured by changed lives. We ought to witness increasing love, integrity, and character that resembles Jesus.

Repeatedly, transitions come to congregations and they do not survive them. What happens when a pastor moves away, falls into sin, retires, or dies in most Christian churches? Within two years the church has either descended deeply into debt, become stagnant, or been so dramatically altered by new leadership that a new congregation must be raised.

Sunday after Sunday we leaders preach at our congregations, telling them what they ought to do, how they ought to behave, how much they ought to give, etc. We seldom *show them.* Crew members of the *Titanic* were never shown how to lower a lifeboat. They were never shown how to lead small groups in lifeboats. They were never taught the rudimentary elements of seamanship. Instead, they were taught to simply obey orders. Obeying orders required very little of the crew. It meant to simply be where the captain or his representative required them to be and do exactly what they commanded. Many pastors are quite happy with this leadership style as well, but it has little to do with biblical Christianity!

Disciples are Jesus-lovers. Leaders are stewards of these precious gifts, and our mission is to help them discover and deploy their spiritual gifts while developing the character of Christ. Preaching and teaching plays a part in that development, but modeling is the most efficient New Testament means of imparting life and training church members. Effective leaders show the way by personally discipling others and deliberately creating opportunities for others to do the same.

We all know in our heads that effective disciple-making is a modeling, intimate, care-giving experience. In our practice however, we prefer to continue in the traditions that produce clones of ourselves rather than disciples of Jesus.

Churches may appear strong and healthy on the outside because members have learned the Pavlov principle of obeying orders to serve God. The church will be clean and freshly painted. The flowers will be perfectly in place. The songs will be of the highest quality, but it will resemble the *Titanic* — magnificent to look at and businesslike in operation, but deadly. We measure fruit in crises when relationships (or lack thereof) are tested. Those built solely on loyalty to the leadership will fail.

All the crewmen of the *Titanic* were dependable to a point, but few were trained seamen. When Captain Smith summoned his "loyal" crewmen back to the *Titanic* to pick up more passengers, they were faced with a choice. They could obey the captain and risk danger to save more lives, or they could ignore him and preserve their own necks. Their solution to the current crisis was to row far enough away from it to be safe. The greater the distance, the less they would hear cries for help. Quartermaster Hichens in boat #6 echoed the sentiments of everyone: "No, we are not going back to the boat. It is our lives now, not theirs."[1] Spiritual application: "Forget about reaching lost people, they're probably going to hell anyway. Let's focus on our own troubles."

On many lifeboats, crewmen, out from underneath being "ordered" around, chose instead to elect themselves miniature dictators. Now they were in command, so passengers became their new subjects. This is reminiscent of the Pharisees: "They tie up heavy loads and put them on men's shoulders, but they themselves are not willing to lift a finger to move them" (Matt. 23:4).

While passengers aboard each lifeboat learned to familiarize themselves with new surroundings, the bow of the *Titanic* sunk further and further beneath the waves. Eventually the tragedy took its course with the stern rising high above them. The lights went out amid the cacophonous sounds of screaming people and crashing equipment. Then the ship split in two, and for a few moments the stern section returned to normal. Some actually thought the *Titanic* would still be saved, but moments later the stern section rose again to finally plunge beneath the waves as hundreds jumped into the freezing waters of the Atlantic.

Panic seized the survivors. Many feared the suction of the great ship would pull them under as well. This unusual blending of humanity began to row furiously, striving to remain afloat. The danger however, was past. All that remained was a dark ocean and suffering people.

Within moments, each lifeboat assumed its own

unique identity and accompanying characteristics. While we find it difficult to comprehend how these survivors could virtually ignore the screams of several hundred people, we need to understand something. Each boat had already begun to operate under the philosophy of operation they had learned. Crew members did not abandon pride with the loss of the ship. It developed and spread aboard each lifeboat under a different name. Self-preservation became the new battle cry. They, too, could pick and choose who would live and who would die.

Pleading by some passengers to return and pick up victims fell on deaf ears in every boat, save boat #4, which picked up five crewmen.[2] This newer and smaller leadership community put into practice what they had learned: "Every man for himself!" Hundreds more might have survived if crewmen had opened their hearts in compassion and been courageous. But self-preservation is not a characteristic of courage.

The philosophy of ministry in *Titanic*-like churches produces after its own kind. Apprentices raised in these systems learn to fear the face of man. Under the watchful eye of authority figures, they jump through the hoops of superiors with little regard to pleasing the Master or caring for the legitimate needs of the lost. This training in men-pleasing eventually transforms apprentices into hypocritical little Hitlers when these same authority figures are absent.

When Jesus commissioned us to go and make disciples (Matt. 18:18-20), He didn't mean just any disciples. The Pharisees had followers as well (Matt. 23:15). The disciples we are commissioned to make, however, are to live like, and resemble Jesus. Good fruit are disciples willing to put aside their agendas to serve others for the sake of the gospel. Everything else is chaff.

Eventually, the survivors had the wisdom to link up with other lifeboats to help further stabilize their situation. It was only a matter of minutes before a great many drifted into despair, losing hope of ever being saved. Six hours previously, some of these same passengers danced and laughed in the warmth of an ocean liner ablaze with light and sound. Now, several of them were widows facing bleak futures.

God's Standard

The prophet Amos had an experience that might be an appropriate way to conclude our remarks about the *Titanic* thus far. In Amos 7:7-8 we read: "This is what he showed me: The Lord was standing by a wall that had been built true to plumb, with a plumb line in his hand. And the Lord asked me, 'What do you see, Amos?' 'A plumb line,' I replied. Then the Lord said, 'Look, I am setting a plumb line among my people Israel; I will spare them no longer.' "

Plumb lines, profoundly enough, are made of two components: the line, (usually string), and the plumb (a weight with a point on one end). When a carpenter attaches one end of the line to the top of a wall, the plumb falls to within one inch of the ground. The plumb wags back and forth, gradually becoming perfectly still. The plumb is pointing to the earth's center of gravity, thus producing an accurate vertical line. If the line is 1/4 inch from the top of the wall, but 1 1/2 inches from the bottom of the wall near the plumb, the structure is dangerously crooked. A builder may "eye-up" a wall and pronounce it to be straight, but the plumb line will authenticate his claim.

God warned the people of Israel that He was setting

a plumb line among them. They had measured their righteousness by their own standards. Through Amos, the Lord established that His standards were the only true measure. The Jews thought they were doing well, but God's plumb line of judgment would reveal how flawed their righteousness really was.

Christians have also developed certain standards of righteousness and holiness in the Church that do not measure up to God's. What we label success and achievement, God often judges as vanity and emptiness (Luke 16:15).

The lifeboats (fruit) of our churches will be tested by God's plumb line of truth and judgment. "For it is time for judgment to begin with the family of God; and if it begins with us, what will the outcome be for those who do not obey the gospel of God?" (1 Pet. 4:17). The numerical size of a congregation, their recent success, or their financial power appears to suggest God's favor, but the character of leaders that are raised is a more accurate measure. The Lord is examining our work to see what type it is. Paul the apostle expressed it this way:

> For no one can lay any foundation other than the one already laid which is Jesus Christ. If any man builds on this foundation using gold, silver, costly stones, wood, hay, or straw, his work will be shown for what it is, because the Day will bring it to light. It will be revealed with fire, and the fire will test the quality of each man's work (1 Cor. 3:11-13).

The gospel of Jesus Christ is different than the gospel we have become drunken with in the West. Ours is a gospel majoring on personal rights and minoring on the pre-eminence of Christ and His will for our daily lives.

A woman aboard one of the lifeboats, for example, claimed the title of Christian. After the rescue, she sought to comfort other passengers with her faith, saying, "You women, why do you cry for your husbands? My husband is gone, but I know he's saved." Moments later however, she made another discovery and cried out in anguish, "But all my jewels are gone! All my jewels!"[3] As pathetically absurd as this seems, she exemplifies the sort of fruit our gospel has produced: profoundly religious, but self-centered and oblivious to the Day of Judgment. Paul preached a gospel that included our individual appointments at the Judgment Seat of Christ (Rom. 2:16; 2 Cor. 5:10).

Titanic-style churches are out of touch with what God values. I believe that His plumb line of truth has already been dropped, exposing Western Christianity as "wanting," in many cases. Booking passage aboard the *Titanic* involved a choice based on personal values and needs. We also have a choice and do well to be skeptical of Christian organizations which exude the same philosophy of pride, image, and greed that the *Titanic* manifested.

Down through history, the first generation of any revival is usually characterized by zealous preaching combined with miracles and dramatic conversions. The second generation of that revival generally consists of the first generation's children. The preaching typically remains doctrinally correct, but is less intense and more management-oriented. By the third generation carnality frequently sets in, with people more conscious of what society thinks of them than what God's Word teaches. By the fourth generation, the values of the original movement have been replaced by a tepid but comfortable religious facade, ". . . having a form of godliness but deny-ing its power" (2 Tim. 3:5).

Jesus said that our fruit is to remain. I understand fruit to be the work of God in people. He holds little in-terest in preserving our movements. God does care deeply, however, that each generation is reached. To accomplish this, we must become committed to investing ourselves in tomorrow's leaders today. God's plumb line is designed to show the workman where he has gone wrong so that he can make corrections. If we'll listen, the church Jesus promised He would build will be finished! (Matt. 16:18.)

Other ships played significant roles in this tragedy. All have stories to tell and vital spiritual principles to relate.

Questions for Reflection

1. The validity of any philosophy or ministry is proven by what measure? Is your church bringing the lost to Christ?

2. Passengers aboard the *Titanic* viewed her as in-vincible. How does this parallel the condition in many churches?

3. "There exists a subtle but very deliberate belief that our programs or services are the primary means through which salvation is to occur." Why is this be-lief dangerous to the future of the Christian church?

4. What does this statement mean: "A success with-out a successor is a failure"?

5. What is a plumb line? What reason did God have for bringing it among His people?

Chapter 5

Playing It Safe

Not long after Captain Smith discovered that his command was doomed, crew members sighted another ship less than seven miles away. Fourth Officer Joseph Boxhall told the Board of Trade inquiry that he first saw the light of a ship near the *Titanic* while returning from the bridge. Using binoculars, he distinctly sighted two of the ship's masthead lights.

At approximately 12:45 a.m., Boxhall fired the first distress rocket. He continued doing so at five-minute intervals with Quartermaster George Rowe's assistance. Boxhall observed the mysterious ship approaching. Soon her red port sidelight and starboard lamp became visible without using binoculars.

Other people, including the captain, saw the lights as well. Smith ordered Boxhall and Rowe to try contacting the vessel with the Morse lamp, which they did between firing rockets. Both men judged the ship to be between four and six miles away. The Countess of Rothes claimed to have seen a tramp steamer.

No response came from the other vessel. It appeared to ignore the blaze of distress rockets coupled with the light of a powerful Morse lamp. Worse still, she seemed to be turning slowly.

Before Boxhall left the *Titanic*'s bridge (about 1:40 a.m. to join #2 lifeboat), he saw only the vessel's stern light, at two points off the *Titanic*'s bow. In spite of their efforts, the other ship seemed uninterested in helping them and began to sail off.

Earlier that evening, Stanley Lord, captain of the *Californian*, made the decision to double his lookouts. Their proximity to ice was nothing to fool with in his opinion. He took charge of the bridge a few minutes after 8 p.m. Accompanying the captain was Third Officer Charles Groves.

By 10:15 p.m., Lord became convinced that the illuminated western horizon was caused by ice. The captain was no risk-taker. He ordered his ship to a full stop. It would not get underway again until 5:15 a.m. the next morning.

At 35, Stanley Lord had become a captain with the Leyland Line six years earlier. His 6,233-ton ship, one-seventh the size of the *Titanic*, was carrying cargo from Liverpool, England, to Boston, Massachusetts. No passengers were aboard.

Leaving the bridge at 10:30 p.m. to go below, Captain Lord spotted a light to the east. It captured his attention enough to point it out to Third Officer Groves. Lord judged it to be an approaching vessel.[1] Groves thought it was a star.

When the captain returned to the bridge around 10:55 p.m. he asked wireless operator Evans if he knew of any other ships in the vicinity. "Only the *Titanic*," he replied. "That's not the *Titanic*. She's closer to us in size. You'd better contact the *Titanic* anyway and let her know we're stopped in ice."[2] Evans immediately set to work contacting the *Titanic* with the message, ". . . stopped and surrounded by ice."

John Phillips, the senior wireless operator aboard the *Titanic*, was exasperated from overwork and rudely insisted that Evans "shut up." Nevertheless, the *Californian* operator continued trying to warn the *Titanic* for more than 30 minutes. Finally, Evans gave up — 10 minutes before the collision.

By 11:30 p.m. the starboard light of the mysterious ship was plainly visible to the crew of the *Californian*. Estimating the distance to be five miles, Lord commanded the ship to be contacted by Morse lamp. There was no response.

When the watch changed at midnight, Lord asked the relieving officer, second officer Herbert Stone, to advise him if the nearby vessel came any closer. He told Stone that he would be resting on a small sofa in the chart room and left the bridge.

To Stone the vessel appeared to be starboard of the *Californian*. He observed one masthead light and a red sidelight: also one or two indistinct lights resembling open doors or portholes. He also judged her to be a small tramp steamer about five miles off. Like Groves did earlier, Stone repeatedly tried to reach the ship via Morse lamp, but found no success.

Around midnight, fireman Earnest Gill came on deck after completing his 8-to-12 watch. Having just come from the lighted engine room, Gill blinked his eyes against the night's darkness as he leaned over the starboard rail of the *Californian*'s upper deck. Peering into the night, Gill saw ". . . a very large steamer, about ten miles away. I watched her for a full minute. . . . She was going at full speed." Gill went below but was unable to sleep. He left his bunk and went up on deck again about 12:30 a.m. He had been there for about ten minutes when he saw a white rocket ". . . about 10 miles away on the starboard side. I thought it must be a shooting star. In seven or eight minutes I saw distinctly a second rocket in the same place. . . . It was not my business to notify the bridge or the look-outs. . . . I turned in immediately after."[3]

On the bridge, Second Officer Stone also had observed a flash of light in the sky at 12:45 a.m., the *Californian*'s time. At first he thought it was a shooting star, but a short time later he viewed another light, directly over what he judged to be a small steamer, appearing to come from a good distance beyond her. Between that time and about 1:15 a.m. he witnessed three more lights, the same as before and concluded that they were "white rockets," a sure sign of distress at sea.

At 1:15 Stone whistled down the speaking tube to advise Captain Lord of the successive white rockets. Answering from his own cabin, Lord inquired if the rockets were company signals, Stone replied, "I don't know, but they're all white." Lord ordered Stone to continue signaling the nearby vessel via Morse lamp, and ". . . when you do (get an answer), let me know by Gibson." Again Stone signaled the ship without response. The captain returned to the chart room sofa. Had the *Californian* used her wireless to identify the mystery ship seen by her captain and officers, she would have heard the *Titanic*'s distress call.[4] For the next 45 minutes, three more rockets were sighted.

Meanwhile, the *Titanic* was sinking fast. Lifeboats descended the ship's side, but not before the crew instructed those on board to row immediately toward the red light in the distance. That red light surely meant a ship that would save everyone. Those attempting to reach the mystery ship later testified that their efforts were fruitless since the ship began moving in the opposite direction.

The *Californian* drifted on the ocean and by 1:50 a.m. was heading west-southwest. The other ship had a bearing of southwest-by-west and around 2:00 a.m. had begun steaming away, bearing southwest 1/2 west. Her red portside light became invisible, and only her stern light could be seen.

As ordered, Stone sent apprentice Gibson to report to the captain. Gibson returned, saying he had told the captain not only of the ship's departure but also of the sighting of eight distant rockets. According to Gibson the captain acknowledged his report and then asked about the rockets: "Are you sure there were no colors in them?" He replied, "No, they were all white."[5] Lord then asked him the time and, after telling him, returned to the bridge to report to Stone.

The captain went back to sleep until he was awakened by the second officer reporting that he could see no more lights and that the ship was out of sight. The *Californian* did nothing. The captain slept in his cabin from 12:40 a.m. until 4:40 a.m.

Cyril Evans had one thing in common with Captain Lord: he, too, was fast asleep. Refusing to listen to his warning, the *Titanic*'s wireless operator, Jack Phillips, frantically tried to manage the backlog of messages from passengers to Cape Race. Evans took off his headphones, shut down his apparatus, and went to bed. The mechanically-operated detector was unwound, and therefore incapable of responding to the distress calls that soon began crackling through the night.

At 4:00 a.m., Chief Officer George F. Stewart replaced Stone on the bridge. Alarmed by the events of the previous watch, he woke the captain and Evans. Within moments, Evans picked up a message from another ship

Stanley Lord, captain of the *Californian.*
(*Courtesy of Titanic Historical Society*)

The *Californian*, cruising the disaster area on the morning of April 15. The crew of this ship has been vilified through the years for failure to answer the *Titanic*'s distress calls and rockets. *(Courtesy of National Archives)*

that the *Titanic* had struck an iceberg and was sinking. Even then, Lord refused to act, waiting until the light of dawn before commanding the *Californian* to head toward the *Titanic*'s last reported position.

Following zigzag courses between south and southwest, the *Californian* pushed through the ice, never exceeding six knots. Reaching open water about 6:30, the ship proceeded at full speed — 70 revolutions, or about 13 1/2 knots — southwards, down the ice field's western edge.

When they arrived at 8:00 a.m., another ship, the *Carpathia*, prepared to leave the scene with the *Titanic*'s survivors safely onboard. The *Californian* came up alongside the *Carpathia* offering to take some of the survivors, but the captain refused. Instead, he sent a message to Lord asking him to stay in the vicinity and pick up any bodies. The *Carpathia* then steamed away, bound for New York.

The *Californian* supposedly searched the area for an hour or so and continued toward Boston. "Lord's ship found no bodies. One can only conclude that he did not search very hard since days later, the Mackay-Bennett, out of Halifax, still managed to pick up some (306 bodies)."[6]

Stuck in a Paradigm

Stanley Lord went down in history as a coward. Both the British and American inquiries following the disaster concluded that Lord failed to come to the rescue of the *Titanic*'s passengers. The crew of the *Californian* might have been heroes. Instead, the newspapers portrayed them as villains, citing Captain Lord's negligence as the reason hundreds of people perished.

Like the *Titanic*, the *Californian* represents a philosophy of operation that is prophetic in scope. The *Californian* was enmeshed in a paradigm — a way of looking at the world — which closely resembles the way certain church members and their leaders have learned to respond to those around them.

The *Californian*'s philosophy was built upon the fear of rejection. Lord was an extremely cautious man. At first glance, we might gather that he was prudent and wise. Doubling lookouts and staying sharp was certainly a better strategy than running full-speed into icebergs. As the night unfolds, however, we see a man so completely terrified of disaster that nothing (including the loss of hundreds of lives) would motivate him to change his extremely cautious behavior.

After learning of the *Titanic*'s trouble, Lord refused to do anything until daylight. "The lackadaisical attitude of the *Californian* crew is beyond comprehension. . . . Rationalization is a popular shield for cowards. Were they so afraid of the ice that they decided to humor each other with unbelievable reasons for not responding to the obvious emergency?"[7]

Lord must have perceived early in life that taking risks increased the possibility of failure. Reaching out to other people might invite rejection — even ridicule. The captain sought to minimize his losses by cautiousness and withdrawal.

Overbearing and aloof, the captain was not one to inspire confidence. Leadership was merely a job for him. Involving himself in the lives of the men who served under his command in all probability never crossed his mind. It is doubtful whether anyone really knew him or the insecurities he lived under. To this commander, developing relationships and inspiring new leaders were not on his "To do" list.

To be part of the *Californian* crew was not a particularly rewarding experience. What do you suppose it would feel like if your entire worth was based solely on what you did, rather than who you were as a person? It may not be that hard to imagine. Many church members already feel that way every Sunday morning!

Morse lamps were one method of communicating on the high seas, but the Marconi wireless helped ships speak to each other much more effectively, and over longer distances. Lord relied upon the Morse lamp to contact the other ship. When it did not respond, he ceased trying to communicate. Later, Stone tried contacting the same ship with the same method with the same results. Had Cyril Evans been awakened to use the wireless, the crew of the *Californian* might have heard the *Titanic*'s distress call and changed history.

The philosophy of operation based on fear permeated every facet of life onboard ship. Taking advantage of new opportunities in communication would be irrelevant to a leader like Captain Lord. He was not responding to changes in the world, because he viewed the world around him as a threat. Fear locks people into antiquated habit patterns. We continue on in the old ways because we are afraid of the new.

Churches aren't much different. A survey of a typical, Evangelical church in the United States or Europe would reveal a number of antiquated methods of communicating the life-changing message of the gospel. Some services are like stepping into a time-warp. The music is either 100 years old (That's what makes it sacred!), or so overused it is laughable (Let's sing, "This Is the Day" one more time!). So many Christian churches follow the same order of service week in and week out, yet criticize traditional churches for being ritualistic. Look at our gatherings! They are every bit as predictable. Service begins a few minutes late, followed by a half-hour of songs. Sit down. The offering is next, then announcements you will forget a few minutes later. Finally, the piece de resistance: the sermon, preaching the gospel to the same crowd that stopped listening long ago.

We have perfected form at the expense of life. The Church has slept while the world changed. We, like the *Californian*, have the potential to save the perishing, but we are too fixed upon methods that worked when God anointed them long ago. Have we emphasized a particular method above the *life* of the message?

Jesus' ministry was radical. He wasn't bound to a synagogue. Most of His sermons were outdoors. Jesus did not care about all the externals we get nervous about. His focus was discipling, blessing, feeding, and releasing people to their respective destiny with His Father. Much of His teaching took place on streets, in homes, on the way to town, and sitting under trees. He wasn't stuck in old methods. He preached from fishing boats, taught in wheat fields, healed on Sabbath days, and ministered to outcasts rejected by the religious systems of the day.

"It's Not My Job"

Fear of rejection affected nearly every crew member on the *Californian*. Most acted as spectators; seeing the problem, but unwilling to risk their reputations to do something about it. Consider the testimony of Fireman Earnest Gill who spotted two distress rockets: "It was not my business to notify the bridge or the lookouts." Why wasn't it his business? Did Gill's personal troubles prevent him from caring enough to sound an alarm? He knew white rockets indicated distress. How did he conclude his sighting was none of his business?

Consider the same prevailing attitude of many American Christians: apathy. How many believers genuinely care for the welfare of their leaders or the church itself? Church attendance is considered just that: *attendance*. Becoming a part of the team ("One for all and all for one!") is foreign to us. Instead, we elect to be armchair quarterbacks when things go wrong. ("You know, if I were leading the church, I wouldn't have let that happen," or, "They should've let the Sunday school director go a long time ago.") We have excellent hindsight, but little vision. Anyone can fix mistakes after the fact, but God is looking for individuals willing to risk being a part of a team. Being related to other people will bring pain, but it will also bring progress to the kingdom of God.

What spawns apathetic behavior? I believe apathy begins with the belief that our actions will have little impact. No matter what we do, people and events will remain the same. Church members buy into this attitude through unresolved authority and bitterness issues.

God is a God of resolution. Temptations cannot defeat us unless we let them since, "No temptation has seized you except what is common to man. And God is faithful; he will not let you be tempted beyond what you can bear. But when you are tempted, he will also provide a way out so that you can stand up under it" (1 Cor. 10:13). Trials of our faith cannot neutralize us unless we permit them to, for "Who shall separate us from the love of Christ? Shall trouble or hardship or persecution or famine or nakedness or danger or sword? . . . Neither height nor depth, nor anything else in all creation, will be able to separate us from the love of God that is in Christ Jesus our Lord (Rom. 8:35,39).

Christians become apathetic when they do not reach out to God during times of hardship or personal pain. They learn to cope instead of overcome. Coping takes many forms. The most common form (exemplified by Stanley Lord) is to withdraw. We hide from potential or perceived conflict. Other coping mechanisms include blaming others, slandering reputations, competition, or outright hatred. Millions of Christians throughout the world choose to cope with hardship this way. They read of God's desire to help them overcome but learn to disbelieve it because of discouragement, and what is discouragement but dependence upon ourselves for solutions.

Jesus provided a scriptural mechanism for resolving bitterness in the local church — Matthew 18:15-17: "If your brother sins against you, go and show him his fault, just between the two of you. If he listens to you, you have won your brother over. But if he will not listen, take one or two others along, so that 'every matter may be established by the testimony of two or three witnesses.' If he refuses to listen to them, tell it to the church; and if he refuses to listen even to the church, treat him as you would a pagan or a tax collector." Verse 20 reveals that prayers will be answered only after relationships between brothers and sisters are restored.

Related to this are issues of authority. Failing to recognize Jesus behind the authorities in our lives dooms us to confusion, disappointment, and despair since some of these very people are God's messengers of guidance. Failing to submit ourselves to Christ by honoring the authorities He has selected for us is a failure to honor the

Father himself. We see these authorities as unmovable obstacles to success. Therefore, we develop coping mechanisms to deal with defeat. Eventually, we become apathetic, believing that God never comes through.

Fear Engraved In Stone

In *The Ship That Stood Still,* author Leslie Reade gives us insight into some of the personal dynamics aboard the *Californian* which influenced decision-making that fateful night. Second Officer Herbert Stone was one of the men who sighted distress signals coming from the mysterious ship. Few realized how deeply he was affected with fear and rejection issues. Due to a neurotic fear of a domineering father, he had fled from home at age 16. These unresolved problems with his parent governed the way he dealt with other authorities placed over him. A man of average character, for example, would have disregarded Lord's orders and insisted action be taken, but Stone was afraid. The overbearing Lord was too much like his own father and Stone thought better of placing himself in jeopardy, opting to remain paralyzed in fear.

Spiritual leaders who suffer feelings of rejection tend to attract people to their churches who possess the same weakness. When a leader withdraws from others because of a fear of rejection, others with the same dysfunction frequently join the church where they can be accepted among peers. Rather than forgiving and accepting healing, members of the congregation withdraw from healthy Christians and relationships to attract to those of like woundedness. They learn to live with an undercurrent of bitterness, cutting themselves off from God who promised to forgive our trespasses in the same manner we forgive others.

Stone witnessed the need but waited and waited.

Inner conflict grew to the point when he could stand it no longer. He would have to confront the captain, but due to the lack of relationships and trust of each other, Lord ignored him.

Counting the Cost

Surviving pain is a part of being a disciple. It is not a badge to wear excusing us from reaching out to others. I encounter Christians daily who have been "wronged." They've learned to "play the game" and conceal their anger well with a contrived pleasantness.

I have heard it said that trials make you bitter or better. They make you bitter when you have vested interests to protect. They make you better when you thank God for them and trust the Holy Spirit to "work all things together for good" (Rom. 8:28).

Jesus promised that all of us would experience hardship (John 16:33) and Paul promised the same to his young apprentice (1 Tim. 2:3). Many of us, however, do not plan for trials to come through other Christians! In the final analysis, what is the difference? Pain is pain no matter where it comes from. We have two options when it comes: cope with it somehow or overcome it altogether.

God's purpose for the believer is to overcome. Overcoming always involves humbling ourselves and asking for help. Through humility, we necessarily invite other people into our lives for assistance, correction, and nurture. We risk being hurt again, but the alternative is remaining under the bondage of bitterness.

Many leaders and churches have been through storms, but have not grown stronger or wiser for the experience. Their response to adversity has been withdrawal. Laziness and apathy replaced risk-taking. Having been hurt through former problems, leaders learned to stop when trouble comes and wait for circumstances to improve. This sort of self-protection is what cowardice is all about. It takes guts to care. It takes courage to face rejection and misunderstanding.

What keeps good people from responding to real need? Oftentimes, it is the fear of rejection or apathy. We can be alarmed at the degradation we witness every day, but remain immobilized by fear. Apathy keeps our minds occupied long enough to dull the effect of our consciences. This insidious combination neutralizes the Church, making it easily defeatable by the forces of darkness.

The *Californian* carried no passengers. In church terms, she was not reaching the lost. The *Californian* churches have allowed fear and apathy to cause them to lose sight of their purpose and mission. Nothing attracts people to the church or the church to people. Those aboard simply function, performing their respective duties as expected. The *Californian* churches are oblivious to the lost. Those aboard are "safe," but not blessed by God with new converts.

How many church members cry out to God for growth and impact on society with few, if any, results? Ask yourself: Would God entrust new converts to churches steeped in fear and apathy? Would He entrust disciples to leaders with no vision and lacking in the ability to die to self? Of course not!

A Friend in Need

At the inquiry following the tragedy, crew members helped condemn the captain. Apprentice James Gibson was a key witness who testified against him, relaying to the world how his leader had chosen to sleep rather than investigate obvious distress calls. Lord's neglect in developing friendships and teamwork with his men cost him dearly. They turned their backs on their captain, intent on seeing him bear the entire blame.

Relationships within the body of Christ can be just as two-faced. On the surface we call each other "brother" or "sister," yet in reality we haven't the slightest idea of the pain going on in each other's lives. Paul instructed us to "Rejoice with those who rejoice; mourn with those who mourn" (Rom. 12:15). Such a condition presupposes that Christians live in community together; that is, that they care for and look after each other as fellow members of the body of Christ.

It is not uncommon to see two distinct and dichotomous relationships among many Christians. There is the church relationship, in which we embrace and communicate our love to each other during a Sunday service. Then there is the real relationship, when we spot fellow believers in the supermarket and go down another aisle hoping they did not see us!

When Christians carry on this way, the world is not impressed. Jesus taught us, "By this all men will know that you are my disciples, if you love one another" (John 13:35). Love one another? Most believers don't even *like* one another!

Our methods have tended to focus on doctrine to the exclusion of all else. Yet, what made Jesus' teaching so powerful was not only its inherent truth, but its context. There simply isn't Christianity without a deeply personal relationship with God and equally personal relationships with fellow believers (1 John 1:7).

Repentance Without Pain

Stanley Lord always maintained that he was innocent. He said the ship the *Californian* saw that fateful evening was not the *Titanic* but a small steamer. He and others believed that the British inquiry, led by Lord Mercy, railroaded him as part of elaborate efforts to protect White Star's interests.

Captain Lord tried unsuccessfully on at least two occasions to clear his name. Seventy-eight years after the accident, his son succeeded — partly. Due to new evidence that had come to light when the *Titanic* was discovered in 1985, the transport secretary ordered a re-examination of the case on July 9, 1990, and it was finally published on April 4, 1992.

Their conclusions were both good and bad for Captain Lord:

> — The *Titanic* and the *Californian* were 18 miles apart, not 7 as had been charged.
> — It is possible that the *Californian* could not have arrived at the *Titanic*'s accident site in time to save the survivors. The first rocket was sighted at 12:45 a.m. If they had gotten immediately underway, they might have reached the sight just after she sunk, but not in time to take people from the ship.
> — The engine room should have been placed on immediate alert by ringing, "stand by engines."
> — The wireless operator should have been called.
> — Captain Lord, after being called by Mr. Stone, should have gone to the bridge and gotten the ship going toward the rockets.

The newest inquiry did not completely exonerate

Stanley Lord. He remains an example of inept leadership controlled by fear, who ultimately had his own interests in mind and by so doing became a lifelong object of contempt.

The inquiry also reported the very real possibility that another ship was in fact nearer the *Titanic* than the *Californian*.

After publicity surrounding the sinking died down, Stanley Lord lost his command but was later rehired by the Nitrate Producers Steamship Company, enjoying a prosperous working relationship for several years. The *Californian* was sunk by a torpedo during World War I.

Questions for Reflection

1. What was the philosophy of operation aboard the Californian built upon?

2. Why is over-cautiousness and withdrawal lethal to a church?

3. How does apathy develop?

4. Is being part of a team essential in advancing the kingdom of God?

5. How does our unwillingness to admit mistakes affect our daily lives?

Chapter 6

The *Samson*

Was the *Californian* the ship the crew of the *Titanic* saw? Not likely. Witnesses from both the *Titanic* and the *Californian* testified that the mystery ship was moving, and we already know that the *Californian* stopped dead in the water from 11:00 p.m. on. With the passing of time, and armed with fresh insight from Ballard's research, it is all but certain that Captain Lord's assertions were correct; there *was* another ship, but who was it?

A number of possibilities have been advanced, which included ships like the *Virginian*, the *Mount Temple,* and the *Thistledhu.* All are possibilities, but one stands out as the most credible. The Norwegian Television Authority revived a story recently claiming that a sailing vessel, the *Samson,* was in the vicinity at the time of the accident.

Captain Henrik Naess, who was serving as the chief officer at the time, claimed to have seen the *Titanic*'s lights and distress signals, but had turned away from them. He made these statements many years after the disaster.

If the facts corroborate, the *Samson* is perhaps the most heinous of all the ships we have examined yet. She alone would be responsible for the hundreds of screaming men, women, and children who froze to death in the icy waters of the Atlantic that fateful night. How could a captain and crew of any vessel deliberately forsake so many of their fellow human beings during such a desperate time?

The answer may be discovered by exploring the purpose for which the *Samson* was in the Atlantic late that night to begin with. Captain Naess and his crew sailed the cold Atlantic late at night for a reason: an illegal one. They were hunting seals, a practice expressly forbidden by international law.

If we believe the claims of both the *Titanic*'s survivors and Captain Lord, the ship they all witnessed was approximately seven miles away. If the *Samson* was the "mystery" ship, the Naess' crew would have been capable of seeing the *Titanic* clearly, since she was ablaze with light until her last seconds.

Initially, the *Titanic*'s presence in the North Atlantic was not perceived as a threat to Naess's illegal activities. She was miles away and seemingly disinterested. Suddenly, the *Titanic* stopped. This must have alarmed the crew. It was extremely unusual for an ocean liner to abruptly stop in the water so late at night. The captain reasoned, perhaps, that the *Titanic* was merely correcting a minor problem.

One hour passed. White rockets shot up into the sky, illuminating the mammoth ship below. The *Titanic* signaled the *Samson* with a Morse lamp. Several miles in the opposite direction, another Morse lamp (from the *Californian)* flashed out a signal, too. *They were discovered!*

With hearts pounding and chests heaving in the night air, the *Titanic*'s former passengers rowed with all their might towards the mysterious ship in the distance. The more rigorously they pulled on the oars, the further the ship appeared to move away.

Captain Naess understood what white rockets meant, but getting arrested was far too high a price to pay. He ordered his men to turn the ship away from the *Titanic.* The one ship with the greatest opportunity of saving people steamed away, ignoring international distress calls to save their own skins.

Meanwhile, Stanley Lord was left to shoulder the blame for the tragedy despite his contention that the *Californian* was positioned 17 to 20 miles from the *Titanic.* The ship they had seen was not the *Titanic,* he asserted, but a much smaller steamer. No inquiry probed deeply enough to agree. Coupled with the damning testimony of his own crew members, Lord wore the badge of "guilty" the remainder of his life.

Hirelings

Jesus loves people. In John 10:1-14, He illustrates just how dear His people are to Him. In these verses, Jesus refers to himself as "the gate" through which all sheep must enter to have relationship with God. He then refers to himself as "the good shepherd." Jesus knows the sheep and they know Him. He willingly lays His life down for them, suggesting that good leaders do the same.

Jesus also speaks of those who are hired hands — other kinds of church leaders. About them Jesus tells us they are thieves and robbers, abandoning the sheep at the first sign of a wolf. He adds, "The man runs away because he is a hired hand and cares nothing for the sheep" (John 10:13).

Sad to say, but like every generation before us, we do have hired hands leading some churches. It would shock you to learn just how many individuals have pursued and then entered the ministry — some with university degrees — having no love for people.

For some, the ministry furnishes an opportunity for power and control over other people. They utilize a title like the Pharisees as a means of hearing "Reverend" or "Pastor" before their name. Some enter ministry as a means of getting affirmation from people. They study hard in seminary to learn how to say pleasant things so that people will say and think well of them.

Pastoring has its rewards. There certainly is nothing quite like preaching an anointed sermon to a spiritually hungry gathering, or counseling a marriage back from the brink of divorce. There is joy when you know that your contribution helped change a life for the better. More often than not however, pastoring is also a painful vocation, calling individuals to lay aside their personal comforts to bear burdens with people.

The difference between shepherds and hired hands is relatively simple. Shepherds serve out of love for the flock. Hired hands serve for what they can get out of it. Recognition, social status — even money — can be the hidden reasons people set their goals to become clergymen. Such individuals are the most pathetic of all, disgracing the cause of Christ to feed their own appetites.

A number of years ago, while working in a restaurant, I encountered a minister like this. He exhibited a proud spirit, striving for recognition. Whenever he saw me, he peppered his conversation with "Praise the Lord!" His boisterous proclaiming of Christian phrases did not sit well with me. My spirit did not bear witness with his faith. My unsaved boss tried to get us together, knowing we both were in the "religion game."

Eventually, I had to tell my boss about my reservations, and to my surprise he agreed with me! I did not discern a man who cared for God's people.

I still remember the day my boss informed me that this man had left town with his secretary, leaving his wife to care for their eight children! This is not to suggest that every man who morally fails is a hireling. Our righteousness is based on faith in Christ's blood. I am attempting to establish, however, that hirelings, like the tares among the wheat, do exist in today's Church. Sooner or later the wolf shows up to test the mettle of every minister. Under pressure, hirelings forsake the sheep in order to pursue their own pleasure.

The *Samson* represents churches led by leaders who serve Christ for the wrong reasons. These are churches that have "a form of godliness but deny its power" (2 Tim. 3:5). Their philosophy of ministry centers around self-gratification and personal gain. Leaders in such churches have no consideration for what is ethical or godly, but what is profitable. They seek to pacify their flocks with the newest program or most titillating social concern, oblivious to God's will for the Church.

As with the *Titanic* and the *Californian,* philosophies of ministry produce after their own kind. None of the crew argued with the captain or tried to change his mind about staying. As a leader he was engaged in wrong behavior and those desiring to be free of moral responsibility were attracted to him for that very reason.

Jesus charged the Pharisees for their "*Samson*-like" behavior in Matthew 23. He said of them:

— They did not practice what they preached (v. 3).

— They burdened men with loads they were unwilling to carry themselves (v. 4).

— Everything they did, they did for men to see (v. 5).

— They loved the place of honor and to be greeted by titles (v. 6-7).

— They struggled to make converts who became twice as bad as themselves (v. 15).

— They practiced tithing but forgot justice, mercy, and faithfulness (v. 23).

— They appeared righteous outwardly, but were full of hypocrisy and wickedness (v. 28).

The *Samson* might have saved people. All she needed to do was stop what she was doing, accept responsibility for her actions, and help the less fortunate. Instead of the worst cowards, the *Samson*'s crew could have been international heroes.

We're all *that* close to doing great things for God. The *Samson* is God's way of showing us the worst man can do with the opportunities He grants. Without His grace, we are a most despicable people, likely to throw aside what is important in order to gain the praise of men. However, we are always only one prayer away from forgiveness, cleansing, and salvation.

If only some other ship with a more responsible crew were so close, many more might have been saved! Yet God, in His wisdom, chose *Samson*. God entrusted lawbreakers with a wonderful opportunity to change direction and become heroes. When Jesus offered Judas the sop of bread at the Last Supper, He was offering him *honored guest status*. He appealed to Judas' conscience by this loving act, knowing which direction he would choose. In a similar way, God offered the *Samson* the best shot at saving the survivors of the *Titanic*. They could have recognized their selfishness, forsaken their temporal profits, and become a force for the salvation of many. Unfortunately, like Judas, the crew of the *Samson* chose their own interests.

God, in His mercy, still presents even the most wicked of churches opportunities to repent, be cleansed, and become useful in saving souls. It isn't fair by human standards, but thankfully God doesn't check with human standards before acting! His arm is not shortened to take the most worldly congregations and transform them into shining beacons of righteousness. The key is always humility. "Oh, the depth of the riches of the wisdom and knowledge of God! How unsearchable his judgments, and his paths beyond tracing out!" (Rom. 11:33).

Few of us can imagine what it must have been like to be a crew member of the *Samson,* knowing your ship could have helped the *Titanic* — how it might feel to remember the tragedy every day for the rest of your life, realizing you let people die to save your own skin. It might almost have been better to die with the *Titanic* than betray those in need and have to live with it.

The story of the *Samson* might end here, were it not for another interesting turn of events. The captain of the *Californian* would be hounded with accusations the rest of his life, but Naess and the crew of the *Samson* were never charged with anything. They only had their consciences to wrestle with. Since the ship was unknown, she was never implicated. No one ever learned of the criminal behavior of the captain and crew until years after they died.

As fate would have it, the old *Samson* was sold. Her name was changed to *City of New York*. A great irony exists in this move. The new owner, oblivious to the *Samson*'s past, chose to name her after the city where she might have delivered the *Titanic* survivors, had Naess been more courageous. The new captain loved the little wooden ship, but it would never be used again for criminal acts. He had a much nobler plan for the 512-ton ship. She was not quick of speed or brand new (1885), but the *Samson* was the one ship a notable man searched the entire globe to find. With its 34-inch thick timbers, the *City of New York* would become a vessel of honor and renown, for her new captain was no less a figure than Admiral Richard E. Byrd, the famous explorer of the Antarctic!!

Paul encouraged his good friend and ministerial associate, Timothy, "In a large house there are articles not only of gold and silver, but also of wood and clay; some are for noble purposes and some for ignoble. *If a man cleanses himself from the latter,* he will be an instrument for noble purposes, made holy, useful to the Master and prepared to do any good work" (2 Tim. 2:20; emphasis mine).

Though it is not common, wayward churches CAN change. They do not deserve God's grace (Who does?), but He still holds the option to sovereignly extend mercy to a handful of self-centered congregations that He may be glorified. Do I understand that? No. I don't understand the atonement either, but I'm glad I can enjoy it!

I know of one fellowship fitting this description. It was forsaken by almost every godly Christian. Those leaving all but pronounced it "dead," and incapable of ever being used of God again. God sovereignly over-ruled — against the advice of many of the Christians in the area! Reason dictated that the bitterness, apathy, and abuse of authority demanded the final judgment of God. Instead, He chose to send in a new leadership team.

Over the next few months, the "doomed" church was winning the lost. Today it is a thriving congregation. I point this out, because it needs to be said: God can do what He wants! If mercy can be extended, expect Him to find a way to do it! If a congregation develops a heart to be instruments for noble purposes, God's grace can and will restore a church, not for the reputation of the church, but for His own glory.

Well, the time has come to examine the most incredible part of the *Titanic* story. The ship we will discuss next emerged from the tragedy as the hero. The captain and crew exemplified some of the finest seamanship and Christian character ever witnessed on the international scene. Her name was *Carpathia*.

Questions for Reflection

1. The *Samson* was given the best opportunity to help the *Titanic*. What does this tell us about God?

2. How can wayward churches be turned around?

3. What are hirelings?

4. What is the maximum amount of time a sinner is allowed to keep transgressions hidden?

The real mystery ship? Pictured here around 1930, after it had been renamed the *City of New York* (and purchased by polar explorer Richard Byrd), the *Samson* saw the *Titanic's* distress signals, but failed to act. *(Courtesy of the Mariners' Museum, Newport News, Virginia)*

Chapter 7

The *Carpathia*

Fifty-eight miles away from the *Titanic*, a Cunard ship, the *Carpathia*, was cruising east to the Mediterranean at 14 knots.[1] Their trip had been uneventful and it seemed as if it would stay that way.

The *Carpathia*'s wireless operator, Harold T. Cottam, felt exhausted, having been on duty since 7:00 a.m. During his watch he had overheard Jack Phillip's snub to Evans, the *Californian* wireless operator. Afterward, he had changed over from the shipping wavelength and listened to the news from Cape Cod, Massachusetts.

He began to slowly undress, kneeling down to unlace his boots. It was now past midnight. Harold's shift was over and the receiver should have been shut down, but he wanted to have some fun before turning in. Cottam switched on his transmitter and tapped out MGY (the *Titanic*'s code letters), receiving in reply, a hasty "K" ("Go ahead").

"Good morning, old man. Do you know there are messages for you at Cape Race?" he tapped out lightheartedly.

Out of the night came the dreaded letters of the international distress call: "CQD CQD SOS SOS. Come at once. We have struck a berg. Position 41.46 N., 50.14W. CQD SOS!" Harold wasted no time conveying the message to H.V. Dean, the officer of the watch. Dean did not wait for repetition.

At 12:35 a.m. both men burst into the captain's quarters to report that the *Titanic* had struck an iceberg. Arthur Rostron, the 43-year-old commander of the *Carpathia,* was a bit miffed. He had been sleeping soundly, and did not appreciate this loud interruption. As Dean's words began to take hold, he asked for confirmation from Cottam.

Hurriedly pulling on his uniform, Rostron ascended to the bridge and consulted the navigation charts. A 27-year veteran of the sea who had served as chief officer aboard the *Lusitania,* Captain Rostron acted decisively, summoning all the resources his training would afford him. No detail escaped his attention as he prepared the *Carpathia* for the most important mission of her career.

The 13,564-ton *Carpathia* wheeled around to head northwest on her new course. Alerted by the bridge, the engine room officers and crew began building pressure in the ship's 10-year-old boilers.

As the *Carpathia* surged forward, Rostron assembled his officers and issued a series of orders to prepare the ship and her crew for receiving survivors. One of the many heroic acts performed that night, Rostron's commands were textbook examples of preparation and foresight. Issued under the great pressure of the moment (it was after midnight), they demonstrated superbly the master's knowledge and skill.[2]

Because it was late at night, many of the *Carpathia*'s passengers would not awake until the drama had been played out. Rostron had specifically instructed his crew that as much as possible, silence should prevail. Passengers seen walking around were instructed to return to their cabins and stay there.

Aboard ship were three doctors. The English doctor was directed to the first-class dining room to prepare for survivors. The Italian doctor was directed to his new office in the second-class dining room, and the Hungarian doctor would set up his practice in the third-class dining room. All supplies necessary to treat the sick or injured were hastily but meticulously prepared and rushed to each room.

Other crew members received orders to use their skills in further preparing for their expected guests. The chief steward, for example, was to have hot coffee, soup, drinks, and blankets ready for those rescued.

Rostron ordered all gangway doors opened, assigning officers to learn the names of survivors to inform relatives quickly. Others prepared block and lines with chair slings for the wounded. Canvas ashbags were positioned for hauling up the children. Nets and portable lights were strung along the sides of the ship. Bowlines were secured along the ship's sides along with boat ropes and heaving lines for lifting people in chairs. Ladders were readied. Not one detail escaped the captain's eye — even the task of pouring oil down the forward lavatories to make the surface of the sea outside as smooth as possible.

Meanwhile, the *Carpathia* was increasing speed as the ship set out on her 58-mile journey. This was a dangerous mission; after all, they were heading into a region that had already proved deadly for the "unsinkable" *Titanic*. What made the *Carpathia*'s captain so confident he wouldn't experience the same fate? In the words of Captain Rostron:

Into that zone of danger we raced the *Carpathia*, every nerve strained watching for the ice. Once I saw one huge fellow towering into the sky quite near — saw it because a star was reflected on its surface — a tiny beam of warning which guided us safely past. If only some such friendly star had glistened into the eyes of the look-out on the *Titanic*. . . . Ah, well, it was not to be.[3]

At 2:45 a.m., Second Officer James Bisset saw the first iceberg. They steered around it and kept going. The next hour they dodged five in all.

More and more now we were all keyed up. Icebergs loomed up and fell astern; we never slackened, though sometimes we altered course suddenly to avoid them. It was an anxious time with the *Titanic*'s fateful experience very close in our minds. There were 700 souls on the *Carpathia*; these lives, as well as all the survivors of the *Titanic* herself, depended on a sudden turn of the wheel.[4]

Reducing speed was out of the question, but the captain took every measure to reduce the risk to his own ship and passengers. He added a man to the crow's nest, put two more on the bow, and one on each wing of the bridge for a total of seven lookouts. Before the night was over, the ship would comfortably exceed her registered 14-and-a-half-knot top speed, achieving over 17 knots.

Into the night the *Carpathia* surged forward toward destiny. Unlike Stanley Lord, Rostron was not sleeping below. He stood alone on the bridge where one might expect to find him. Second Officer James Bisset remembered glancing over at the captain during one instance to witness his head bowed in prayer.[5]

Beginning at 3:00 a.m., the captain ordered company rockets to be fired in 15-minute intervals in the hope of reassuring the *Titanic* or her survivors. As they approached the *Titanic*'s last called position, the lifeboats were sighted. At 4:10 a.m., they began picking up survivors, which proved to be a difficult task. The sea had lost her calmness.

As the sun rose it revealed an astonishing sight; the sea was full of icebergs for as far as the eye could see in all directions. Even with all the lookouts the *Carpathia* had passed numerous icebergs which they had not even seen. No one could imagine how they missed them all except their pious captain.[6]

He later said, "When day broke, and I saw the ice I had steamed through during the night, I shuddered, and could only think that some other Hand than mine was on that helm during the night."[7]

By now, many of the *Carpathia*'s passengers had awakened due to all the additional bustling about. Learning the terrible news, they didn't waste time talking to each other, but offered themselves in a way that far exceeded expectations. Picking up the spirit of self-sacrifice from the crew, many began helping to feed and provide medication to the survivors. Every man gave up his cabin for a stranger. Some of the women doubled with others to free up their own quarters.

> There was absolutely no excitement. . . . The ladies were very soon self-appointed nursing sisters, getting the newcomers to lie abed,

others to rest on deck, and doing what they could to ease suffering and console. As many of the second and third class passengers who came aboard were but poorly clothed, blankets and sheets were requisitioned and many of the ladies started to make clothes. Others went to the third class and busied themselves nursing, clothing, and feeding the children. The cream of human kindness was surely extended that morning and during the days that followed while we made New York, and through it all that quietness reigned.[8]

The *Californian* arrived just after 8:00 a.m., wiring the *Carpathia* of their willingness to help transport the survivors to New York. Rostron refused this first of many requests by other ships to assist. He did not want to further traumatize these men, women, and children by unboarding and reboarding another ship in the middle of the Atlantic.

Before heading back, Rostron couldn't resist one last look around. It occurred to him that a brief service might be appropriate. So he sent for Rev. Anderson, an Episcopal clergyman onboard. Passengers and crew from the *Titanic* and the *Carpathia* assembled in the main lounge to remember the dead and give thanks for the 705 who had been saved.

At 8:50 a.m. the *Carpathia* turned toward her new course and sailed away. The journey home would not be without obstacles, however. Almost immediately, Rostron found his way blocked by a huge ice field stretching as far as he could see. This was the field described by the *Mesaba*'s ice message Sunday night — the message that failed to reach the *Titanic*'s bridge.[9]

Clearing the ice field, the *Carpathia* then ran into that other great enemy of ships at sea — fog. They were not to be completely free of this menace until the trip was over. Making matters worse, as they came near the United States coastline, a violent storm broke out complete with thunder, lightning, boisterous winds, and torrential rain. Each new obstacle challenged the mettle of everyone aboard ship.

External difficulties were not the only menace. Charles Pellegrino, in *Her Name: Titanic,* notes that cardsharps (gamblers sailing under assumed names) found their way off the *Titanic* and onto the lifeboats. By their clever scheming aboard the *Carpathia*, these men stung the *Titanic*'s survivors for up to $30,000. They were never caught.[10]

As the rescue ship neared the coastline, newspaper reporters executed several bold maneuvers in their attempts to get exclusive stories from the survivors. Rostron was firm in his conviction that none be permitted on his ship. Nevertheless, one did manage to climb aboard, but did not achieve his objective. The captain requested the reporter honor his wishes about interviewing the newcomers. To his credit, the man obeyed.

When the *Carpathia* finally arrived in New York Thursday night, the rain was still coming down. The first stop was the White Star pier to deliver 13 empty lifeboats to their rightful owners. Next, Rostron brought the ship to its own Cunard berth where the passengers disembarked at nine o'clock.

Nearly 30,000 people stood in the rain, anxiously awaiting news of their loved ones. Joyous reunions eventually gave way to sobbing and wailing from those who knew they would never see their friends or relatives again. In a few hours, they all gradually disappeared into the darkness.

Now that the *Carpathia* had accomplished her mission, she resumed her journey to the Mediterranean. After restocking and refueling, she steamed away from New York — exactly one week from the time of their previous sailing.

The following day, the *Mackay-Bennett* was dispatched with the unenviable task of retrieving bodies of the lost. They found 316 bodies, and 116 were buried at sea because of extreme damage or decay.[11]

England honored Sir Arthur Rostron, as did President Taft, together with countless others for his bravery and heroism during the *Titanic* crisis. Promoted to the rank of commodore, he served aboard such prestigious liners as the *Mauretania* and the *Berengaria*. His distinguished career won him many other honors before he retired at the family home in Southampton, England.

The *Carpathia* continued serving passengers until WWI, when the ship was used for war purposes. She was torpedoed by a German submarine on July 17, 1918, and sank 170 miles from Bishop's Rock, off the coast of Ireland.[12]

Questions for Reflection

1. What happened when the *Carpathia*'s passengers finally awoke?

2. Who arrived too late, but asked Rostron if any help was needed?

3. To whom did Rostron give credit for the saving

of the *Titanic*'s survivors?

4.. The crew of the *Samson* escaped during the night of the sinking, but was justice ever served? What are ways in which seemingly unknown acts are brought to light in our spiritual lives?

Titanic survivors mingle on the deck of the *Carpathia.*
(Courtesy of Grant Freeman)

Sir Arthur Rostron, captain of the rescue ship *Carpathia*.
(Courtesy of Grant Freeman)

The rescue ship *Carpathia*, as depicted in this period postcard. (*Courtesy of the Titanic Historical Society*)

—*St. Louis Globe-Democrat.*

THE REFUGE

A newspaper illustration days after the sinking.
(Courtesy of Grant Freeman)

Chapter 8

The Church Jesus Is Building

It may seem odd to say, but there are substantial amounts of churches that Jesus Christ did not build. Many churches that began well have left behind New Testament patterns and are now more of an annoyance to Him than an asset!

The *Carpathia* is a prophetic model of the New Testament Church Jesus is building. Their greatness was not in their speed, their size, or their creature comforts. The greatness of the *Carpathia* was in her crew.

The *Carpathia* did the basics well. The philosophy of operation was teamwork. Serving others, even when it involved sacrifice, was considered a joy. Captain and crew viewed themselves as members of a team. The objective was to work together and bring the best out of each other.

Harold Cottam might have considered his function as a wireless operator to be just a job. If he had, 705 more people would have died. Harold was tired, but viewed his contribution as a joy, not a duty to perform. He contacted the *Titanic* out of the goodness of his own heart. There was a certain playfulnesss in his voice, for he did not view the *Carpathia*'s mammoth competitor as an enemy. No trace of jealousy was expressed through his actions — only helpfulness.

There is a grace that exists among churches where Jesus is actually boss. Competition among Christians is a despicable activity fueled by the flesh. God gives gifts to certain parts of His body to accomplish certain things. Too often church leaders look at what everyone else is doing to figure out God's will. Paul taught us that comparing yourselves among others is an unwise act (2 Cor. 10:12). Further, he urged all Christians to learn what God's perfect will is for their lives or risk being unwise and therefore unfruitful (Eph. 3:10; Col. 1:9).

Carpathian-type churches rejoice that others are saving souls, healing the sick, strengthening the Body. "*Carpathians*" see other churches as fellow laborers, "fellow citizens with God's people and members of God's household" (Eph. 2:19). Competition is irrelevant, since their quest is God's glory.

When Cottam learned the *Titanic* was in trouble, he contacted Dean. There was a clear understanding aboard ship of the chain of command. Some reading this might comfort themselves that I am finally reinforcing the place of authority. God has given authority on various levels in the Church, but never does that imply superiority. Far too many leaders have made themselves indispensable in the local church and missed God's exact purposes for giving them authority in the first place.

For example, when I have a toothache, I normally see a dentist. He has the knowledge I lack. Based upon his qualifications, I grant him the authority to make judgments about my teeth. The dentist is not superior to me. He or she functions with a skill that I appreciate and need. If I were to take matters into my own hands, my problem would not only remain unresolved, but would undoubtedly become worse.

In the Church, God has set apostles, prophets, teachers, workers of miracles, those with gifts of healing, administrators, etc. (1 Cor. 12:28). He initiated this to provide maximum blessing to everyone, not exalt certain members to pedestals of power. Cottam was accountable to Dean, and by following that specific chain of command, communication remained clear.

Arriving at the captain's quarters, Dean knocked, but Cottam burst in without hesitation. I personally like the fact that Rostron was annoyed with their interruption. It tells me that the man was not some unreal super captain. Jesus is not building a church where everyone always does everything in a perfect manner. We are, as Lyman Coleman says, "wounded healers." For my money, I don't trust perfect churches. Perfect on this earth speaks to me of machinery, not humans. While we strive daily to become more like Jesus, our humanity remains an integral part of the equation.

With the chain of command in full operation, notice the sequence of events. Rostron heard the message from Dean. He then confirms the message with Cottam. Why? Didn't he trust the officer of the watch, whose duty it was to report irregularities to the captain? Of course he did, but the philosophy of operation aboard the *Carpathia* dictated teamwork all the way. If the captain was to commit his ship, crew, and resources to saving another ship, he needed to be absolutely sure he was getting clear direction. "In the multitude of counselors there is safety" (Prov. 11:14).

The possibility always exists for human error. The more we deliberately commit ourselves to being a team, the better our chances are for hearing and acting according to God's will. Many Christians today commit their time, energy, finances, and futures to causes and concerns that are not upon the heart of the Father. Not enough time is spent seeking all the avenues of counsel designed by God to give us wisdom toward understanding His will. The "lone ranger" approach to guidance is fatally flawed, leading to much activity but little fruit. We need to be committed to those things that are worth dying for.

Captain Rostron did not first look into whether the *Titanic* was a Cunard liner. The issue was irrelevant. He sprang to action while confirming that the facts were indeed the truth. Known for his quick decisions, Roston had a knack for transmitting unlimited energy to those serving under him. Because of this unique talent, he was nicknamed, "the Electric Spark" by his fellow shipmates.[1] That energy was set to be released as never before.

He arrived at the bridge and immediately consulted the navigation chart. Though he had sailed for many years and probably knew the charts forwards and backwards, Roston nevertheless consulted these charts as if he were reading them for the first time. This priority in his life easily parallels the church leader's need to be relying upon God's Word for detailed direction. The church of Christ must be one that reveres His Word.

Vince Lombardi became famous when he transformed a losing football team into a winning one by repeatedly drilling them in the basics. Christian leaders who are not renewed in the Word, irrespective of how many years they have served, will lack the specific direction needed to be effective in helping people. God will not commit His disciples to leaders who have stopped feeding on the bread of God's Word.

Faced with a great need and hundreds of variables, Captain Roston began issuing commands. The first was to turn the ship around. The second was to instruct the engineer to fire up the boilers, making certain all energy was diverted to the engines. All extraneous use of power ceased, while propellers pushed the ship faster and faster. Before the majority of organizational orders were issued, he made his officers know that passengers were to be left out of the planning. Ahead of them were unseen dangers. They didn't need quarterbacking from inexperienced personnel. Besides, they would need the added rest for what lay ahead.

How many churches do you know of today working to bless other churches? Are not most Christians immersed in their own business? Is it any wonder the unsaved are not impressed with the love we have for each the other? (John 13:35).

God has ordained leaders to carry varying degrees of authority. Authority is designed exclusively to bless the church (2 Cor. 10:8). The church is not ruled democratically — or shouldn't be! While on the surface, democratic rule with each member having an equal say appears fair and equitable, it also flies in the face of New Testament principles. The church is not a democracy (rule by majority), but a theocracy (rule by God). God decides what is right, and we position ourselves to obey Him.

If Roston had decided to be democratic, he could have awakened the passengers and devised plans while people died. No, this was not a time to vote and ask opinions. It was a time to call upon the existing gifts and abilities already present.

In the church, leaders must be prepared to make tough choices. This does not mean disregarding members of the congregation, but serving them by keeping them from burdens God has not asked them to carry. The passengers eventually played a vital role in the rescue, but timing and function were key here. The passengers were not qualified to make nautical decisions. Awakening them would create obstacles, not opportunities.

Arthur Rostron models for us what every leader should strive for as stewards over God's house. He coordinated the unique abilities of each crew member toward the care of the hurting. He did not withhold information from passengers to inflate his own sense of importance. He would inform them at the right time and in the right way. When he did, no one grumbled over his decision.

God has appointed leaders in His church to train others to do the work of the ministry (Eph. 4:11-13). This does not mean simply telling others what to do. Training means the personal involvement of a leader with those he is training. It is a discipling relationship, by which trained leaders get to know trainees. This process involves spending time together, sharing the vision of the church, showing how to solve particular problems, extending care in times of need, and helping to recognize and hone the skills the trainee possesses. In a word: time.

Rostron had trained these men. They respected him, not out of fear, but because he was an appreciative leader. They knew he was not self-centered but others-centered. When he was strict, his crew knew it was for the benefit of others. When he delegated a responsibility, it was because he had complete confidence in them.

In many ways, Captain Rostron exhibited the traits seen in our Lord. He led them selflessly, modeling for them the lifestyle of a servant-leader. Was it any wonder that his crew enthusiastically imitated the same spirit of sacrifice they saw displayed in his life?

Both the *Titanic* and the *Carpathia* raced into icebergs, but with different results. God leads humble leadership around icebergs, not into them. The *Titanic* was prevented from seeing ahead, but the *Carpathia* found that the starlight illuminated the path. Proverbs 19:17 records: "He who is kind to the poor lends to the Lord, and he will reward him for what he has done." In Proverbs 2:8 we read "For he guards the course of the just and protects the way of his faithful ones." The Lord adds grace to those who make their heart's desire to serve other churches. The *Titanic* had ignored the cry of the *Deutschland* in her distress. Proverbs 21:13 records: "If a man shuts his ears to the cry of the poor, he too will cry out and not be answered."

Key to Rostron's success as a leader was not only his attention to detail and the full utilization of each crew member's gifts. He was a man of prayer. The captain did not stand on the bridge cursing icebergs. He knew that in spite of his training, in spite of his ship's abilities and the expertise of the crew, they were helpless without God's intervention.

This detail may seem like a given for most leaders, but I assure you it is not. Many of us are lured into believing that our brilliance will carry us through, providing God's anointing in our ministries. Skill development is a good practice, but ultimately, success is hinged upon the presence of God. Without His presence, our labors are empty and pointless.

Prayer is a powerful, yet helpless act. We are placing ourselves at the mercy of our Heavenly Father and abandoning our own efforts. Prayer as a lifestyle is an ego-buster, destroying self-reliance while taking the focus off our puny efforts.

Leaders lead, and while that may not seem profound, God has not called church leaders to disciple from the dugout. Lord slept in his quarters, but Rostron, tired from a full day's work, stood with his men and prayed. Heroes are made of stuff like that.

Modeling our Christian faith creates an ever-widening influence on others. The crew thought of the comfort of survivors because the captain's philosophy of operation was OTHERS FIRST. Personal comfort was at the bottom of his priority list. Saving lives and thinking of the welfare of the lost, (down to the most infinitesimal need) drove Rostron's decision-making process. He was a lover of men, and this attitude subsequently permeated those serving with him.

The crew gladly gave up their quarters — why? Rostron gave up his quarters. The crew went without sleep — why? The captain went without sleep. Like Paul the Apostle, he could easily say, "Therefore I urge you to imitate me" (1 Cor. 4:16). When the passengers opened their cabin doors Monday morning, they heard more noise than they were accustomed to at such an hour. What motivated so many of them to put their own plans aside to serve these strangers? Why did nearly every passenger give up their beds to others — beds, mind you, which they had paid for — to sleep uncomfortably elsewhere on board?

The passengers witnessed the giving nature of captain and crew. It was natural to join in and give of themselves as well. Their possessions became worthless in their own eyes and we begin to see the same heart that possessed one church centuries ago: "All the believers were together and had everything in common. Selling their possessions and goods, they gave to anyone as he had need" (Acts 2:45).

The peace on board came with the security of good leadership. Leon Price writes, "In a church, when every heart is like-minded and the people walk together in a unity of the spirit . . . we can find a place of rest and peace before the Lord Jesus."[2] Leadership sets the pattern under which rest and peace from God will descend upon the church members, or confusion and chaos. This does not mean that there are not times of difficulty, but if tension, burnout, and disorganization are the rule rather than the exception, leadership is not doing the job.

There is favor from God emanating from churches that take risks trying to bless hurting and lost people. The *Carpathia* could just as easily have been destroyed by icebergs. The captain himself knew that in spite of their precautions, only the hand of God had kept them from a similar fate as the *Titanic*. God's sovereignty was at work during this tragedy.

The arrival of the *Californian* had no bearing on leadership decision-making. Captain Rostron had prepared well and by God's grace secured the well-being of all survivors. Subjecting them to further risk aboard an unfamiliar ship made no sense, though he invited the Leyland liner to help by searching for bodies.

The captain was secure in himself. The agendas of other leaders did not send him into intense self-examination. He didn't have a need to cooperate with others so that they might think well of him! Cooperation with another ship had one distinct objective to Rostron: enhancing the welfare of the *Titanic*'s survivors. He politely declined Captain Lord's offer.

Every member of the body of Christ needs to know

who they are in Jesus. We are not who we *think* we are, but who God *says* we are. Paul warns: "We do not dare to classify or compare ourselves with some who commend themselves. When they measure themselves by themselves and compare themselves with themselves, they are not wise" (2 Cor. 10:12). Defining ourselves by comparisons with other leaders/churches/Christians is ungodly. We are called upon to know what the cross of Christ has made us; living, speaking, and acting accordingly.

It is significant that Rostron assembled the entire ship for reflection and thanksgiving to God. The captain was not afraid to lead in worship, correctly displaying gratefulness toward his Lord and reflecting with sobriety upon the price many paid.

Satan was not amused by the actions of the *Carpathia*'s bold captain and crew. There is a price to pay for rescuing the lost, which those chained to pursuing comfort will never understand. When we set our hearts and minds upon blessing others, we invite spiritual warfare. Demons will oppose us whenever we strive to be righteous. This is part of the cost Jesus warned us of before committing ourselves to laboring for Him (Luke 14:28).

Obstacle after obstacle confronted the crew as they attempted to bring the lost to a place of safety. They faced essentially four obstacles, each corresponding to a spiritual principle of Christian growth: icebergs, fog, a storm, and betrayal.

Dealing with Sin

It is not shocking to me that God arranged for the *Carpathia* to see the full dimensions of the ice field that doomed the *Titanic*. What the survivors witnessed was a field nearly 30 miles in width and rising an average of 16 feet above water's surface.

If churches are to do a lasting work of bringing the lost "home," they must be willing to show them the consequences of their former lifestyle. We must not proclaim a cheap gospel that merely rescues us from sin but does not take responsibility for it. True salvation must leave people with no doubt as to their depravity and thorough inability to save themselves. Survivors were shown the full extent and depth of the problem that sunk their ship. Becoming a Christian involves more than adjusting our lifestyle. Following Christ means exercising total repentance that is born of humility. We must acknowledge wholeheartedly that we were doomed because of our own sinfulness and spiritual blindness. Our only hope of escape was God's mercy.

The difficulty many Christians experience in their walk with Jesus is an expectation of comfort built off a wrong premise of salvation. Jesus did not save us to make us feel better. He saved us from hell. Seeing our sin in all its ugliness is a vital step in our salvation. We must confess our full participation in our downfall, renouncing the pride that enabled us to turn a deaf ear to Christ.

The next obstacle the *Carpathia* had to face was fog. Committed to a heroic task, they were now robbed of the nautical sight. The ice field was overwhelming in its enormity. Now Captain Rostron was forced to lead 1,500 men, women, and children in a dangerously overcrowded ship through an eerie fog, further frightening an already exasperated group of survivors. The captain could no longer see where the ship was going. The compass became the central instrument to provide direction.

Paul taught, "We live by faith, not by sight" (2 Cor. 5:7). In other words, our lives as Christians are not based upon external circumstances. We live by faith in God and His Word. All the forces of hell may be attacking our families, our jobs, our finances, our relationships, and our churches, but we cannot rely upon changing circumstances to bail us out. Faith is fixed upon God's power and willingness to act on our behalf. Sight is fixed upon hoping people or things won't let us down, and they always do!

Not long after Christians properly deal with the hideous nature of sin in all of its deceit, God will permit a time of "fog," when we can't "see" God's presence in our lives. Even in this fog, the Lord gives us clear direction: follow His compass (the Scriptures). Familiar surroundings and comforts fall away. It seems as if God disappears as our feelings conjure up predictions of imminent disaster. To come out of the deception of sin always involves the second phase. First, we judge our own sin. Next, we learn to follow His commands irrespective of supporting circumstances. Worldly Christians depend on their senses to get by. The godly learn to trust God's Word when everything is seeming to go wrong.

God is not merely interested in freed slaves, but in adopted sons (Eph. 1:5). We are heirs with Christ positionally and experientially because of faith in His blood. In spite of that fact, our self-centered natures cause us to be prone to deception. The Father longs for us to grow up in Him, strong in the inner man. "Then we will no longer be infants, tossed back and forth by the waves, and blown here and there by every wind of teaching and by the cunning and craftiness of men in their deceitful scheming" (Eph. 4:14).

God is dedicated to raising sons and daughters who learn how to follow Him even when they "feel" lost. He arranges for Christians to go through fog at times, being led only by the previously determined direction for His Word. When the fog began to clear, the *Carpathia* was at her destination. The ship was traveling the correct direction the entire time, because the captain relied on the compass to be trustworthy. Hebrews 11:6 states this principle best: "And without faith it is impossible to please God, because anyone who comes to him must believe that he exists [in spite of circumstances] and that he rewards those who earnestly seek him."

Warfare

Before the *Carpathia* would deliver her precious cargo, another obstacle blocked her path. A violent storm with accompanying winds and torrential rain pelted the weary passengers. This last obstacle speaks of the opposition of spiritual warfare that new believers must face as a regular part of the Christian experience.

Captain Rostron had been through storms before. Weather conditions presented a problem, but did not keep him from staying on course.

Satan hates Christians. That fact is a reality each believer must accept as unchangeable. He will use any means at his disposal to discourage, defeat, and challenge us. The problem he brings against us is no cause for alarm. The greater threat is our reaction to the problem. If disciples give in to fear, discouragement, and reproach, then Satan has achieved his objective.

Jesus said, "In this world you will have trouble" (John 16:33). Paul warned Timothy: "In fact, everyone who wants to live a godly life in Christ Jesus will be persecuted" (2 Tim. 3:12). Peter counseled Christians in this way: "Dear friends, do not be surprised at the painful trial you are suffering, as though something strange were happening to you. But rejoice that you participate in the suffering of Christ, so that you may be overjoyed when his glory is revealed" (1 Pet. 4:12-13).

Storms come to challenge the foundations of our commitment to Christ. Satan is destined to become God's unwitting agent for developing character, perseverance, and stamina in our faith. Through it all, God intends for us to "make it home." The storms are not, as some suppose, telling us we are out of God's will. Captain Rostron knew that. He viewed the storm as an enemy, but an enemy that could be defeated.

The Enemy Is Us

Until now we have discussed external obstacles God allows in order to help us grow and develop in Him — particularly those of us He rescues from prideful church systems. The last obstacle is perhaps the toughest of all. It is not the one easily identifiable through observation. The last obstacle is among us.

On board the *Carpathia* were hungry wolves. Though rescued from certain destruction, no gratitude poured from their innermost being. No repentance for pride occupied their thoughts. Shysters, whose lives were spent offering people "unbelievable opportunities" victimized these hurting survivors for thousands of dollars.

I have never seen a Christian reach maturity without being hurt by fellow believers. Moses had Korah, David had Ahithophel, Jesus had Judas, and Paul had Demas. Face it now: Christians will let you down. Don't protect yourself from this inevitability. Just accept it, and know that God will work character in you through it. We will all be disappointed, suffering loss at the hands of brothers to challenge our faith. This is the most difficult test any of us must experience.

David expresses his feelings over this most difficult of all trials in the Psalms. He was betrayed by his close friend and counselor Ahithophel in a way that directly parallels Jesus' experience with Judas: "If an enemy were insulting me, I could endure it; if a foe were raising himself against me, I could hide from him. But it is you, a man like myself, my companion, my close friend, with whom I once enjoyed sweet fellowship as we walked with the throng at the house of God" (Ps. 55:12). David was a man experiencing deep inner pain.

Betrayal is so devastating because we are seldom prepared. Friendship with others involves letting people into our insecurities. In essence, we become vulnerable by choice. Betrayal wounds us on the inside. Our trust has been violated.

I do not know many Christians who survive this phase. I do know many who *cope* with past hurts, but few who have redemptively learned from them and love the offender. Bitterness is a device Satan uses to rob us of God's grace and transform us into a tool that destroys others (Heb. 12:15). Jesus offers His friends no option except to forgive all who have offended. Forgiveness is real when we can actively bless and attempt to help those who have offended.

Paul warned the Church of "brothers" who would enter our ranks to take advantage of church members (Acts 20:29). Individuals will come among us with other agendas, seeking to take advantage of our kindness for their own selfish motives. Nevertheless, these tragedies are designed to teach us discernment, patience, wisdom, and forgiveness. A wrong attitudinal response will bind believers into a life of disappointment, hurt, and distance from their Heavenly Father. Jesus taught, "If you forgive men when they sin against you, your heavenly Father will also forgive you. But if you do not forgive men their sins, your Father will not forgive your sins" (Matt. 6:14-15).

The shysters aboard the *Carpathia* were never caught (according to Pellegrino). Christian, the one who hurt you may never be judged wrong before men. All vengeance toward offenders must be nailed to the cross of Christ. In the place of bitterness, Jesus calls us to sow love.

Closer and closer the *Carpathia* moved toward her destination. The press (for personal gain) devised a myriad of schemes to get aboard. Rostron thwarted all efforts but one. In the end, no reporter achieved his objective. The Captain models for us a principle of leadership that deserves mention: He refused to allow the praise of men to influence his actions. Gaining approval from the world remained far from his thoughts. Rescuing the lost was the prime objective.

How easy it would have been for him to compromise and grant exclusive interviews to make himself look good. How often leaders and local churches have exchanged the praise of God for the attention of the media. If the Church strives to be recognized by society, she will cease reaching them and become like them. Striving for recognition is pride, which causes God to resist us.

Captain Arthur Rostron was a great man, collecting many honors before his death. His character provides an excellent model of Christian leadership for us to imitate in the Church today. Anyone reading his account of the disaster will be struck by his graciousness, lavishly crediting many others for the mission's success. He was a man governed by Christian principle, unconcerned of personal gain. The church of Jesus Christ in these days badly needs this caliber of leadership.

After making sure his "cargo" was safely home, the Captain went back to his original mission: transporting passengers to the Mediterranean. Rostron would be decorated by England and the United States for his brilliant leadership, eventually being promoted to commodore before he enjoyed a blessed retirement. But for now, he wished to get back to work!

Questions for Reflection

1. The *Titanic* was built by the competition, but that did not matter to Rostron. What does this teach us about the body of Christ?

2. What is the key element in training disciples?

3. Why do you suppose the *Carpathia* crew responded so well to Rostron and how might this parallel God's will for the Church today?

4. What does the *Deutschland* incident teach us about church leadership?

5. The philosophy aboard the *Carpathia* was: Others First. What can we learn from Rostron's example and its effect on the passengers onboard the *Carpathia?*

6. What is inevitable when church leaders determine to reach out and bless others?

7. Part of the maturing process will necessarily involve the enemy from within. When other Christians betray us, what must we do to overcome?

8. The crew of the *Carpathia* used a compass to find the way through terrible weather. What compass can Christians use to weather life's storms?

Chapter 9

"We Can Rebuild Her!"

With the news of the *Titanic*'s disaster fresh on everyone's mind, drastic changes were needed in White Star's newest ship, the *Gigantic*. The *Titanic* had reeked with arrogance, and now the "unsinkable" was sunk. White Star's pride and joy — her almost god-like machine — had been destroyed by an overgrown block of ice. How humiliating!

Britannic was selected as *Gigantic*'s new name, avoiding emphasis on size, and instead basing her strength and reliability more upon national pride than the genius of man's technology.

To assure the public of the *Britannic*'s absolute safety, several modifications were introduced. Harland and Wolff added a new double-hull design. In addition, water-tight compartments were raised above E deck,[1] compensating for the perceived weakness of the *Titanic*. Because of these improvements, *Britannic* would be able to withstand the breaching of six compartments. Psychologically, she could have triumphed where the *Titanic* failed.

With the modifications to her design complete, the *Britannic* was a "better" *Titanic* — at least that is what White Star hoped the public would believe. Helping the worst maritime tragedy in history become a fading memory was the new vision of the company. The triumphing *Britannic* would convince the world that the *Titanic* disaster was just a coincidental mistake.

She was launched on February 26, 1914, with the goal of re-establishing service between Southhampton and New York by the Spring of 1915. When the *Britannic* finished her sea trials, White Star no doubt hoped to regain the respect of the world.

Here was a real chance to recapture the market lost through the *Titanic*. Only one obstacle stood in the *Britannic*'s way: World War I! Before the ship logged a single hour of service, she was requisitioned by the British government to be a hospital ship for the war effort. Instead of transporting rich passengers across the Atlantic, she would transport wounded soldiers back to their loved ones.

Under the command of Charles A. Bartlett, the *Britannic* departed from Belfast on December 12, 1915, headed for Liverpool. Fitted to meet the requirements necessary for a floating hospital, the *Britannic* sailed off to rescue wounded soldiers. On her sixth journey, she was in the Aegean Sea on November 21, 1916, at eight in the morning, when an enormous explosion took place.[2]

A German-built submarine, U-73, had laid mines there one hour prior to the *Britannic*'s arrival. The blast opened 250 feet of the ship to the sea and breached seven compartments! Ironically, the ship sustained damage in roughly the same place as the *Titanic* had almost five years earlier.

White Star's successor to the *Titanic*; the *Britannic* was pressed into service for World War I and was later sunk. *(Courtesy of the Imperial War Museum, London)*

Violet Jessup was probably more alarmed than anyone else. She had traveled aboard the *Olympic* when it collided with the *Hawke*. Escaping that accident unscathed, she later served on board the *Titanic* as a stewardess. Now she served as a nursing sister on the *Britannic*! Ms. Jessup had no trouble finding her way to an available lifeboat!

Within one hour the *Britannic* lay at the bottom of the Aegean Sea. Unlike her sister, she descended in one piece, as was later verified when Jacques Cousteau explored her in 1973. All but 30 people survived the tragedy.

The White Star Line never completely recovered. The *Britannic*'s demise further tarnished their image and forever linked the company with disaster. Over the next few years, it became nearly impossible to recoup the losses. White Star Line was eventually put up for sale in 1927 and almost given away to British ownership. In 1934, White Star was forced by the British government to merge with another shipping company. Who? You guessed it: Cunard — the very company White Star had built their ships to compete against! In the end, it was this fierce spirit of competition that wrecked the company and brought it to ruin.

History Repeats Itself

Printed on the front page of *The New York Times* the morning of April 16, 1912, was a strange statement. It read: **"FRANKLIN HOPEFUL ALL DAY — Manager of the Line Insisted *Titanic* Unsinkable Even After She Had Gone Down."** While we may chuckle over the obvious foolishness of Mr. Franklin, we are nonetheless treated to a glimpse of the paradigm that gripped

White Star management. The *Titanic* cannot sink — even if she has!

Paradigms can become mental idols. Our world view may be so transfixed on what we hope for or dream about that reality is unable to affect us. We can become so convinced that our church is superior to all others or see our doctrines as so invincibly correct that God is hindered from ministering to and through us. Paradigms exist in the minds of many church people, and they can become equally as foolish as Mr. Franklin's.

Titanic churches are destroyed through pride. Humility and repentance are the remedy, but seldom occur. In fact, with the passing of time, leaders invariably attempt to rebuild what God destroyed. Strange isn't it? God judges churches for their pride, but then man stubbornly rebuilds them! After the failures, the splits, the crushed people, and all the rest, the same pride will seek to restore what God has brought down. Modifications will be made, but by and large, church leaders don't swerve from the original model.

In the Old Testament we read of Joshua, Moses' successor. By God's implicit direction, the Israeli people circled the walls of Jericho 13 times. Through a miraculous move of the Holy Spirit, the walls fell down, and Jericho became Jewish real estate. After the victory, Joshua cursed the city however: "Cursed before the Lord is the man who undertakes to rebuild this city, Jericho: At the cost of his firstborn son will he lay its foundations; at the cost of his youngest will he set up its gates" (Josh. 6:26).

God had a problem with Jericho. The evil and degradation practiced there among the inhabitants was so heinous that he instructed Joshua to pronounce a curse upon it from generation to generation. The Lord did not want it fixed or adjusted. He wanted it gone!

When you finish the Book of Joshua, you just know, sooner or later, someone is going to try! You read Judges. No one yet. On through 1 and 2 Samuel. Not a peep. Then, in the latter part of 1 Kings a man called Hiel throws caution to the wind and defies God.

"In Ahab's time, Hiel of Bethel rebuilt Jericho, He laid its foundations at the cost of his firstborn son Abiram, and he set up its gates at the cost of his youngest son Segub, in accordance with the word of the Lord spoken by Joshua son of Nun" (1 Kings 16:34).

Hiel would not accept God's judgment upon Jericho. He thought he had a better plan. He would rebuild the city and make it better than it ever was. God would see. The Lord just didn't understand. Such foolishness cost Hiel his two sons. You cannot build against God. Unless the Lord builds the house, its builders labor in vain. Unless the Lord watches over the city, the watchmen stand guard in vain (Ps. 127:1).

Strongholds must be demolished by those who build them: We demolish arguments and every pretension that sets itself up against the knowledge of God, and we take captive every thought to make it obedient to Christ (2 Cor. 10:5). Pride drives people to build churches to the glory of men. The survivors of church splits must renounce arrogance and self-will or they will inevitably try and rebuild what God has destroyed.

Mr. Franklin's refusal to give up the *Titanic* even though it was destroyed gives us insight into the heart of this organization. This is the company which looked the other way while the Black family attempted to collect money from the widows of men deemed heroes during the tragedy. This is the noble organization which denied compensation to every family of any deceased crew member the moment the *Titanic* sank!

We see in these crass actions a lack of humility or change of heart. Blaming others and expecting payment from the helpless demonstrated the same philosophy that sunk the *Titanic*. Money was not used to take responsibility and care for the hurting, but to strengthen the company. White Star invested its money into the refurbishing of the *Olympic* and the *Britannic* at a cost of hundreds of thousands of dollars.

You see, change only occurs when we judge ourselves guilty and ask for help from God. If He brings our works to nothing, we ought not scheme to start over right away but ask, "What happened?" We cannot imagine the heartlessness of White Star in their treatment of people, but do you know how many times church members are destroyed in church splits and no one ever calls them on the phone? Have you ever known of a church leader who apologized to the congregation for prideful attitudes? It is rare.

Too many times we Christians dust ourselves off and return to the same philosophy that destroyed the last church we were in. Like the *Britannic*, we welcome aboard the old lifeboats (freshly painted to look different) so that we can pretend all is changed.

It is interesting that God intervened, seeing to it that the *Britannic* learned to be a servant by transporting wounded soldiers. The application to the present state of affairs in the Church is obvious. Our destiny is to bless and minister to the wounded. Through this curious turn of fate, the Lord emphasized His call one last time for White Star to learn humility. The *Britannic* would not be the admiration of the world. She would be just a ship among many serving the lowest and most hurting soldier. White Star did not enjoy this change. The *Britannic* was in the Aegean because she *had* to be, not because she *wanted* to be.

One cannot walk away from the *Britannic* without considering her final end. In the same pride which built her sister ship, she was designed to withstand the breaching of six compartments — almost as if White Star was attempting to out-do God. You will remember that the *Titanic* was defeated by an iceberg because up to six compartments were breached. So, the *Britannic* was crafted to overcome such an obstacle.

The mine was laid by Germans, the people who had built the *Deutschland*. The principle of sowing and reaping came to full fruition. Had the *Titanic* sowed by ignoring the need of a German ship in 1912? Now, the *Britannic* reaped an attack by a German submarine. The explosion breached seven compartments. Why not five or six? Was God displaying His judgment for White Star's arrogance? Both liners were built with the human insignia, "indestructible" all over it. Both liners sank when circumstances beyond their control exceeded their capacities to manage the crisis. God prophetically expressed himself. White Star had not learned the lesson.

When God judges a *Titanic* church, it stays judged. Men may plan and scheme, but the final outcome is usually the same. We reap what we sow, and if the philosophy driving any church is pride, destruction will come — repeatedly if necessary — until God is shown thoroughly righteous. I believe that the judgment of God is more responsible for the failing of many churches across the world than satanic attacks. Too many have lifted themselves beyond accountability, in effect challenging God much like Babel of old.

In the end, White Star merged with Cunard. Strange isn't it? White Star executives conceived of three over-sized ships to crush the power of Cunard. When the *Titanic* faltered, who risked their lives to save them? Cunard. Imagine what it must have felt like to sell White Star, far below price, to the company you had spent millions of dollars to destroy. Truly, in that one act, the Scripture is fulfilled: "God opposes the proud, but gives grace to the humble" (Pet. 3:8). Peter is actually quoting Proverbs 3:34: "[God] mocks proud mockers but gives grace to the humble."

Where Do We Go From Here?

As with any prophetic message, we need to step back from it, judge whether it is God, and then heed its message or discard it altogether. The *Titanic* is a warning to the Church. If we persist in building kingdoms God has not called us to build, we will be judged for our arrogance, even though He deeply loves us.

Scripture states: "For it is time for judgment to begin with the family of God; and if it begins with us, what will the outcome be for those who do not obey the gospel of God?" (1 Pet. 4:7). We cry to God for the wickedness and injustice of our society, the child abuse, violence, sexual perversion, and pervasiveness of cults. These all grieve God greatly. His judgment and righteousness is sorely needed. But judgment begins with God's family first. How can He righteously judge the world when His people are filled with pride, fear, and sin?

The *Carpathia* shows us the way God desires to see His church operate. Authority does not have to be power-based in personality. Authority was given to bring God's purposes to fruition. The *Titanic,* the *Californian,* and the *Samson* illustrate for us the way of man. I pray God that we may sign ourselves aboard the right ship!

Questions for Reflection

1. Contemplate the irony of the *Britannic* serving as a hospital ship, and the application to church life.

2. "The *Titanic* cannot sink — even if she has!" How can stubborn paradigms ruin churches?

3. What is the lesson of Jericho?

4. What have your learned about the true nature of the Church through studying these five ships?

5. Since our view of judgment and justice is different from God's, how can we use the story of the *Titanic* to see our Father's plan?

6. As individual passengers on the ship of life, how can we make sure we have booked passage on the right vessel?

Epilogue

One final task that an author must undertake before his or her job is finished, is to proofread the manuscript before it is finally published. It is a tedious job, but the alternative is much worse.

Proofreading *Titanic Warning* was difficult for another reason. I must tell you that the contents of *Titanic Warning* completely convict me in my own behavior. I found myself repenting before the Lord as I proofread each page. It felt as if someone else wrote this book, and I was reading it for the very first time.

The Lord manifested himself in signs that were a wonder to me in the publishing of this book. One noteworthy example came when I finished the rough draft and was faced with the arduous task of seeking a publisher.

During a time of prayer in my cellar one evening, I sensed the Holy Spirit prompting me to spend five days praying and fasting for the manuscript. He impressed upon me that this book belonged to Him, and that I had not been serious enough about getting it published (which was true). I was to pray because there was demonic opposition directed against the book's success.

Ten minutes before my query letter arrived at New Leaf Press, Acquisitions Editor Jim Fletcher was mulling over an idea. *Wouldn't it be interesting,* he thought to himself, *if someone wrote a book contrasting today's church leadership styles with those of the Titanic?* When the letter arrived, he called, asking me to forward the manuscript. Jim called on the fifth day. It didn't take a rocket scientist to perceive that the Lord was moving!

Though the tone of *Titanic Warning* is prophetic and straight to the heart, please know that the message of this book applies to the author as much as (or perhaps more than) anyone else.

May we all humble ourselves and make straight paths for the King of kings, and labor to be His vessels in building His church.

Notes

Chapter 1

[1]Charles Pellegrino, *Her Name, Titanic* (Menlo Park, CA: McGraw-Hill, 1988), p. 129.

[2]Pellegrino, *Her Name, Titanic*, p. 33.

[3]Don Lynch and Ken Marschall, *Titanic — An Illustrated History* (Toronto, Ontario: Madison Press Limited, 1992), p. 102.

[4]Pellegrino, *Her Name, Titanic*, p. 243.

[5]John P. Easton and Charles A. Haas, *Titanic, Destination Disaster* (England: W.W. Norton & Company, 1987) p. 10.

[6]Easton and Haas, *Titanic, Destination Disaster*, p. 13.

[7]Lynch and Marschall, *Titanic — An Illustrated History*, p. 96.

[8]Lynch and Marschall, *Titanic — An Illustrated History*, p. 110.

[9]Pellegrino, *Her Name, Titanic*, p. 185.

Chapter 2

[1]Pellegrino, *Her Name, Titanic*, p. 20.

[2]Rick Joyner, *The Harvest*, (Pineville, NC: MorningStar Publications, 1989), p. 159-160.

[3]Michael Davie, *Titanic, The Death and Life of a Legend* (New York, NY: Alfred A. Knopf, Inc., 1986).

[4]Davie, *Titanic, The Death and Life of a Legend*.

[5]Lynch and Marschall, *Titanic — An Illustrated History*, p. 94.

[6]Lynch and Marschall, *Titanic — An Illustrated History*, p. 95.

[7]Lynch and Marschall, *Titanic — An Illustrated History*, p. 96.

[8]Lynch and Marschall, *Titanic — An Illustrated History*, p. 76.

Chapter 3

[1]Lynch and Marschall, *Titanic — An Illustrated History*, p. 98.

[2]Lynch and Marschall, *Titanic — An Illustrated History*, p. 113.

[3]Lynch and Marschall, *Titanic — An Illustrated History*, p. 100.

[4]Lynch and Marschall, *Titanic — An Illustrated History*, p. 115.

[5]Lynch and Marschall, *Titanic — An Illustrated History*, p. 101.

[6]Joyner, *The Harvest*, p. 159-160.

[7]Davie, *Titanic, The Death and Life of a Legend*, p. 71.

[8]Lynch and Marschall, *Titanic — An Illustrated History*, p. 122.

[9]Davie, *Titanic, The Death and Life of a Legend*, p. 73.

[10]Lynch and Marschall, *Titanic — An Illustrated History*, p. 122.

[11]Pellegrino, *Her Name, Titanic*, p. 241.

[12]Pellegrino, *Her Name, Titanic*, p. 235.

[13]Davie, *Titanic, The Death and Life of a Legend*, p. 79.
[14]Walter Lord, *A Night to Remember* (New York, NY: Bantam Books, 1955), p. 95.
[15]Sir Arthur Rostron, *The Loss of the Titanic* (Wiltshire, England: Titanic Signals Archive, 1991), p. 22-23.
[16]Lynch and Marschall, *Titanic — An Illustrated History*, p. 146.
[17]Davie, *Titanic, The Death and Life of a Legend*, p. 179-180.
[18]Lynch and Marschall, *Titanic — An Illustrated History*, p. 174.
[19]Lynch and Marschall, *Titanic — An Illustrated History*, p. 70.
[20]Lynch and Marschall, *Titanic — An Illustrated History*, p. 70.

Chapter 4

[1]Lynch and Marschall, *Titanic — An Illustrated History*, p. 128.
[2]Lynch and Marschall, *Titanic — An Illustrated History*.
[3]Lynch and Marschall, *Titanic — An Illustrated History*, p. 161.

Chapter 5

[1]Lynch and Marschall, *Titanic — An Illustrated History*, p. 172.
[2]Eaton and Haas, *Titanic, Destination Disaster.*
[3]U.S. Senate Investigating Committee, 1912, inquiry testimony.
[4]Lynch and Marschall, *Titanic — An Illustrated History*, p. 109.
[5]Lynch and Marschall, *Titanic — An Illustrated History*.
[6]Peter Thresh, *Titanic: The Truth Behind the Disaster* (New York, NY: Random House, 1992), p. 65.
[7]Joyner, *The Harvest*, p. 62.

Chapter 7

[1]Lynch and Marschall, *Titanic — An Illustrated History*, p. 142.
[2]Eaton and Haas, *Titanic, Destination Disaster.*
[3]Rostron, *The Loss of the Titanic*, p. 17, 20.
[4]Rostron, *The Loss of the Titanic.*
[5]Lynch and Marschall, *Titanic — An Illustrated History*, p. 142.
[6]Joyner, *The Harvest*, p. 164.
[7]Walter Lord, *The Night Lives On* (New York, NY: William Morrow and Company, 1986), p. 160.
[8]Rostron, *The Loss of the Titanic*, p. 24.
[9]Lynch and Marschall, *Titanic — An Illustrated History*, p. 157.
[10]Pellegrino, *Her Name, Titanic*, p. 237.
[11]Lynch and Marschall, *Titanic — An Illustrated History*, p. 174.
[12]Pellegrino, *Her Name, Titanic*, p. 237.

Chapter 8

[1]Lord, *The Night Lives On,* p. 155.
[2]Leon Price, *Beyond Survival to Victory* (Pleasant Hill, CA: Evergreen Press, 1993), p. 26.

Chapter 9

[1]Pellegrino, *Her Name, Titanic,* p. 188.
[2]Lynch and Marschall, *Titanic — An Illustrated History.*

If you would like information about the Titanic Historical Society, please write to:

> Titanic Historical Society
> P.O. Box 51053
> Indian Orchard, MA 01151-0053

If you would like information about Ken Marschall's prints of the *Titanic* and other ships, please write to:

> Trans-Atlantic Designs
> P.O. Box 539
> Redondo Beach, CA 90277

Casey Sabella considers himself a teacher first, and has a heart for helping pastors and churches work together to see the lost come to Christ. He and his wife, Patricia, have four children. They live in Waterbury, Connecticut.